EVIDENCE for CONVICTION

A DETECTIVE'S JOURNEY INTO EXAMINING THE CREDIBILITY OF THE CHRISTIAN FAITH

RANDAL K. PORTER

Kingdom Publishers

Evidence for Conviction
Copyright© Randal Porter

All rights reserved. No part of this book may be reproduced in any form by photocopying or any electronic or mechanical means, including information storage or retrieval systems, without permission in writing from both the copyright owner and the publisher of the book. The right of Randal Porter to be identified as the author of this work has been asserted by him in accordance with the Copyright, Designs and Patents Act 1988 and any subsequent amendments thereto.
A catalogue record for this book is available from the British Library.

ISBN: 978-1-913247-40-9

1st Edition by Kingdom Publishers
Kingdom Publishers
London, UK.
You can purchase copies of this book from any leading bookstore or email
contact@kingdompublishers.co.uk

To my mother Hilary Porter, you are my creative inspiration. To my sons Keith, Alexander & Jordan and to my grandchildren, Laila, Noah, Elijah, Roman, Eden and Jude, I thank God for you all, and pray that any seeds of faith sown in you, will over time produce a forest of fruit in the saving faith I follow. Finally, to my wife Jean, my life partner, you are my petits pois, I dedicate this book to you all.

CONTENTS

Forward one, by Mike Smith MBE   9

Forward two, by Mike Desousa.   10

Part One
An Evidence-Based Faith

Introduction   13

Prologue: Evidence of God's Grace   22

Chapter 1   Historical Jesus   30

Chapter 2   A Smoking Gun   36

Chapter 3   Corroborative Evidence   47

Chapter 4   Circumstantial Evidence for The Resurrection   53

Chapter 5   Integrity of The New Testament Manuscripts   62

Chapter 6   Evidence of Design   72
               My Journey to Faith

Part Two
A Journey to Faith

Chapter 7	A Need for Answers` Searching	83
Chapter 8	When Trouble's in my Way The Dream	93
Chapter 9	Metanoia Baptism	109
Chapter 10	Doubting and Wrestling with God Wrestling with God	119
Chapter 11	Answered Prayers and Inspiration from a Little Old Lady Sam Kanu's Statement An Evening with Mae Woo	128
Chapter 12	Bible Study: Food for Spiritual Growth The Rich Man and Lazarus A Case Study in Understanding Scripture David and Goliath	140
Chapter 13	Sowing Seeds Faith Sharing Confessions of a Taxi Driver	151
Chapter 14	Closing Statement	159
	Case Notes	167
	Bibliography and Recommended Reading	168
	Unused Material	172

FORWARD ONE

I am deeply honoured to have been asked by Randal to review his book, *Evidence For Conviction*. Firstly I must say that I know Randal to be a sound man of God and one who is unwavering in his faith. It is with this faith that he has stepped out to write about such personal and deep experiences, something most of us only dream about doing.

This book has come at an important time in my life. The very title has challenged my level of faith in many ways. Reading this book, you will find inspiration and encouragement. It will challenge your thinking on the Holy Scriptures, The Holy Trinity, Life and Death, Heaven and Hell.

Once I began reading *Evidence For Conviction*, I found it hard to put down. Every free moment I had, I found myself reaching for this book. Randal has clearly written from the heart as well as a police officer filled with the Spirit of God. If you are not a believer in God, then I challenge you to read this book and remain where you are. If you are already a Christian, then you too can be enlightened and have your level of knowledge increased as you read.

I hope and pray that *Evidence For Conviction* finds its way into schools, colleges, homes and churches worldwide. It is a much-needed resource and a great introduction to the Christian faith.

My prayer for you, dear reader, is that you are blessed beyond measure as you read and search your heart. My prayer for the writer, Randal, is that you pray for inspiration to write a follow up as soon as possible.

All the very best.

Michael Smith MBE

(Founder, Word 4 Weapons)

FORWARD TWO

I can think of many reasons why you should read this book but here are three to be going on with:
1. You will enjoy it.
2. You will benefit from reading it.
3. You will use what you've learned, either to deepen your own convictions or to help others deepen theirs.

I've known Randal for over two decades now and his writing reflects his own character. He writes with honesty, humility and insight. His personal journey is thoroughly engaging.

If you are going to read a book with 'Conviction' in the title then it helps to know that this is something the author is known for!

Randal Porter is a man's man. He's solid in all the right ways; physically, emotionally and spiritually. As a faithful husband, father and friend, he walks the talk, practises what he preaches and leads by example. That's not to say that he is perfect, but rather that he is honest, humble and not hypocritical. A man of great personal integrity, conscientious, consistent and caring. In short, the very qualities you would hope for in a former officer of the law. Randal takes his Christianity seriously and this is reflected in his knowledge and study of the supporting evidence for his faith. In Evidence for Conviction Randal shares very openly from his own life and experience and produces a constructive, captivating and informative read. Using his training as a detective Randal provides us with both the reasons and the reasoning for a robust belief in the Bible and the God of the Bible.

Evidence for Conviction is relevant for seekers, a resource for believers and reassurance for doubters and it allows us to reach a verdict which is beyond reasonable doubt.

Enjoy!

Mike Desouza

Minister of Religion

PART ONE

An Evidence Based Faith

Introduction

At the time of writing, I had spent the best part of seventeen years investigating crime. The business end of what law enforcement officers do is present evidence before a court with the objective of achieving a conviction so that justice can be served. However, there is another meaning for the word, conviction. That deep feeling of trust we can develop that makes us believe something to be true and right. Sometimes that feeling runs very deep indeed, and it is that deep feeling that Christianity is a plausible evidence-based faith, based on historical factual events, that has inspired the title of this book.

A few years ago, I recall having quite a heated discussion with a close relative. Our disagreement was concerning money and the fact that I was contributing part of my income to the church. To many Christians this practice, referred to as tithing, is a no-brainer and we do it without having to think too much about it. However, many non-believers just cannot get their heads around it. This is especially true if giving to the church involves making sacrifices in other areas of expenditure. Like camping holidays instead of flights abroad, or driving an old vehicle instead of a brand new polished car, paid for on finance perhaps.

My relative spoke her mind and accused me of having *blind faith*! What unsettled me about this statement was the fact that she was underestimating why I had faith. The truth is, I know what I believe and why I believe it. This is not *blind faith*. However, my relative's comment exposed a shortcoming on my part. It exposed my failure to share the reasons and the grounds for my faith in God, to those closest to me.

I remember as a teenager, attending Upton House Comprehensive School in Hackney. My Games teacher was a former professional footballer whom I looked up to. I recall we struck up a conversation about God. He informed me he was a Christian.

I asked him how he knew that there was a God. A perfectly reasonable question you would think. His answer disappointed me. He patted his chest with his hand and softly said, "I just know it, I feel it inside." This answer was uninspiring to me. I needed a lot more. A warm feeling inside was never going to be enough to satisfy me that there is a God. I would say that my P.E. teacher displayed something more akin to *blind faith*.

I have written this book with two types of people in mind. The sceptics, who perceive that the Christian faith lacks hard evidence, and the Christians who feel they struggle to have faith. A positive driving force in writing this book is to explain to the readers (hopefully my family members will be amongst the first) the grounds for the Christian faith. To refute the notion that Christianity is a blind faith. I have chronicled my journey; how I arrived at my position of faith in the existence of God, and a belief that the Bible is the revelation of God to mankind.

Firstly, the Bible predicts the birth, life and death of Jesus in the Old Testament. Secondly, it documents His birth mission and teachings in the New Testament. I have tried to demonstrate how an inquisitive search for answers grew into real faith in God, and how that faith has developed and grown to a point where the custodian of the faith, is convinced beyond reasonable doubt that he has found the truth.

Something that possibly sets this book aside from other books about faith is that it is written from the point of view of a police detective, and presented evidentially (part one). To this end, I hope to demonstrate that Christianity is an evidence-based faith. The narrative is the fruit of a quarter of a century of practising Christianity, studying the Bible and three years of directed research into Christian apologetics and church history on a course organised by a teacher in the Thames Valley Church of Christ, Malcolm Cox.

Malcolm and I first met shortly after my conversion in 1992. He started what he termed the School of Missions a few years ago. His vision was to equip Christians with sufficient knowledge to be effective in sharing their faith and converting non-believers. *Evidence for Conviction is* a biographical apologetic study. In it, I invite the reader to join me on a journey (part two) where I detail how I came to believe in God and why, throughout my Christian life, my faith has grown. I wrestled with the idea of separating the biographical side from the apologetic side and write two books. I decided to run the two strands together. For me, my faith is a double-edged sword, the overwhelming evidence I have studied has been tremendously faith building.

James, the brother of Jesus, made a very profound statement in his letter that is preserved in the New Testament. "Faith without works is dead." (James 2:26) My view is that the transformational power of God's Word in my life, those faith building life experiences as I have walked the Christian path are of equal value to my faith and an important testimony to the power of the Bible. It claims to be the Word of God, so if that claim were true, one would expect the words contained therein to have a significant impact on those who read it and embrace it.

The evidence and the journey go hand in hand. Hence, for me, the two strands must be detailed together to fully understand the grounds for my confidence that there is a loving God, revealed in the Bible, and that Jesus is exactly who he claimed to be, the Messiah, the son of God. Hopefully the biographical nature of the book will be inspiring to followers of the Christian faith, my family of believers, and the Apologetics side of the book will be of interest to those curious about the evidence on which we Christians base our faith.

Apologetics is derived from the Greek word, *apologia*, meaning reasoned defence. It is the discipline of defending the Christian faith. Christian believers have a long history of having to defend themselves, dating back to the very first century. Starting with the Apostle Paul who so eloquently defended himself before Festus and Agrippa, as detailed in the book of Acts, which follows immediately after the four gospels. Acts chronicles the establishment of the Church after the resurrection.

The earliest example of an extra-biblical apologist, was Justin Martyr, a genius teacher of his time who was beheaded along with six friends and fellow apologists for Christianity, for the crime of Atheism.

Atheism under Roman rule was to fail to embrace the authorised senate-sanctioned *religions* of the Roman Empire. The following statement from another renowned apologist, Tertullian of Carthage, somewhat encapsulates the sad plight of Christ's followers in the first centuries of the AD era.

"If the Tiber reaches the walls, if the Nile does not rise to the fields, if the sky does not move or if the earth does, if there is famine, if there is plague, the cry immediately goes up: 'Throw the Christians to the lion!" What, all of them to the lion?'

It is fitting that, at the time of writing this introduction, I am only a couple of months short of my 25th anniversary of becoming a Christian. I believe the publication of a book about faith will be an appropriate *fruit* of my three years of directed study, after a quarter of a century of practising my faith and studying the Bible.

I started writing this book in December 2016. At the time, I was eight months into an eighteen-month, career break from the Police Service where I was employed as a Detective Constable. I joined the Police on 2nd December 2002 aged thirty-eight. I have been involved in many serious investigations including murders. I have taken countless cases to court. I ask a lot of questions when speaking to witnesses and suspects during my investigations.

Nothing I am told is taken at face value; I delve deeper and ask further questions. 'The devil is in the detail' is a philosophy amongst good Investigators. I adopt the same strategy towards my reading of the Bible, and what I hear preached from the pulpit. Studying the Bible is a bit like being an archaeologist. You need patience and you need tools. I have several tools that I use to dig with. I will name them now. Who, What, Why, When, Where, How. These tools have served me very well over the years as I have striven to understand the Bible.

Although I take great pride in having served as a police officer for well over a decade, it is not my work that defines me. The biggest defining factor in my life has been my journey in the Christian faith. Part two is inspired by two conversations I had years apart that I have never forgotten. These conversations have shaped my thinking and inspired me to share my faith with countless others as the years have gone by.

In the early 1990s, I was working as an Advertising Sales Executive for my local newspaper. I was not yet a Christian. I remember my manager, Mark, speaking to me about work. He was talking about having lots of potential sales pending and feeding these leads into an imaginary pipeline. He was not a Christian and our conversation was in the context of prospecting for new business. I recall him giving me a pep talk.

Mark was a bit of a 'likely' lad, he had a great sense of humour full of quips and puns. I distinctly remember him saying that, "If you plant enough seeds you will end up with a forest." He thought at the time he was training me on how to be a successful sales person. He was unaware that there was a spiritual connotation attached to what he was telling me. To be honest, I do not think I was even aware at the time.

> If you plant enough seeds, you will end up with a forest

A year or two later, I had just pulled up into the car park at Alexander Palace on my way to a big church meeting at the illustrious venue; a special invitation Service. I recall that far from looking forward to the meeting, I was feeling a bit downcast and even contemplated going home before the service began. I doubted myself. Doubted God would work in my life. Feeling guilty at my lack of faith, and insecure at what I perceived a lack of evidence of the Holy Spirit working in my life. I certainly was not expecting a visitor at this Alexander Palace meeting; otherwise, I am sure I would have been feeling a lot more upbeat. I remember my negative contemplations were interrupted by a young man who approached me. The conversation as I recall it went something like this.

"Excuse me, are you Randal?"

"Yes."

"Hi, do you remember me? My name is Paul." (Not his real name, which is lost to me)

I did not recognise him and my blank expression and sheepish silence as I searched my memory was broken when Paul said the following.

"A couple of years ago you approached me in the car park at

Sainsbury's in Whitechapel. You reached out to me and I never ever forgot what you said. Well, I just wanted you to know that I am a Christian now and I am a part of the Church in North London."

We thanked each other, shook hands and parted company.

Suddenly I was not quite so downcast. The spring was back in my step! I wasn't so useless after all, and in a small way, God had used my feeble efforts to help somebody on his path to salvation. I do not believe for a single moment that it was by coincidence I met with Paul when I was thinking of returning home. I believe God made an exception and arranged our meeting for my encouragement as He had a plan for me. That plan did not involve me quitting the faith.

I say made an exception because I believe that if we were made aware of all the occasions where our outreach and words have impacted people, we would be in danger of becoming proud and conceited.

These two conversations have had a profound impact on how I share my faith. I have a *sow as you go* approach and trust that God will work after I have shared my faith with others. I enrolled in the School of Missions course with the intention of deepening my knowledge of the Bible. However, I got so much more than I bargained for. As I studied, I was astounded at the weight of evidence supporting the person of Jesus and the integrity, of the Bible.

By integrity, I mean trust that the Scriptures have been accurately transmitted down the generations giving the present day reader, an exhibit with outstanding continuity, uncontaminated with doctoring and false information. This study had the effect of both deepening my knowledge of the Bible while at the same time acting as fertiliser for my faith, which has grown so much.

Why choose *Evidence For Conviction* as the title? I adopted this title because the book is about a journey through evidence. It explains how a seed of belief, planted many years ago, grew into an unshakable confidence in the existence of the very God detailed in the Bible. This unshakable confidence is based on credible evidence, enough evidence to kindle my increasing faith.

It is said of some people that they have great faith, and of others, they have little faith, or their faith is weak. Jesus once despaired of his disciples *"Oh ye of little faith."* (Matthew 6:30) This quotation has been used by many over the centuries with reference to any perceived lack of belief. Real faith can be a rare thing even amongst religious leaders. Faith in God is not something we are born with, furthermore, it is not something that we wake up one morning and suddenly have in abundance. Faith is nurtured. However, there is some good news for the Christian who wants more faith.

Firstly, there is no necessity for bucket loads to be effective. Jesus once remarked to his disciples that if they had a mere mustard seed of faith they would be able to move a mountain. (Luke 17:6) The second bit of good news is that if you are proactive in taking part in faith building life experiences, then you can cultivate your faith and make it grow and blossom like a fruit bearing-plant. Faith is an area where we can truly reap what we sow in life.

I once read a book that had me gripped as soon as I saw the title. *If You Want To Walk On Water Step Out Of The Boat.* No doubt, the inspiration for the title was the Apostle Peter. He was the only disciple to step out of the boat on that scary occasion on choppy waters when Jesus himself walked across the lake and Peter stepped out of the boat and attempted to reach him. After a few tentative steps where he did walk on the water, panic set in and he lost his nerve. (Matthew 14:22-33)

Soon after that, he really crashed and burned, losing faith again even to the extent of denying he knew Jesus, three times on the night of his capture and imprisonment. (Luke 22:54-62) Nevertheless, Peter never gave up and returned to the fold to become one of the early church leaders, becoming the source for the gospel of Mark, which is often referred to as Peter's gospel. He also has two letters immortalised in the canon of the Bible.

I must confess that it is the prospect of seeing God's supernatural power working in my life that spurs me on to stretch myself to step out of my comfort zone. Writing a book about faith, for me, demonstrates a remarkable growth in my own belief in God since my conversion to Christianity in 1992.

One reason I was so determined to write this book is that I consider myself average. I am not a super-evangelist, leading a large movement. I am not a preacher, teacher or pastor, leading a large congregation. Just little old ordinary me: average height, average intelligence, unremarkable.

The whole 'being average' thing really became apparent to me one day at Hendon when I was undergoing my police training. I always considered myself to be quite tall. Having a two to three-inch *afro* during my teen years helped a lot, as this gave the impression of extra height. However, once I reached Hendon there was no more *afro*. During a drill, shortly after we had been issued with our police uniforms, we were instructed to line up in height order. My heart sank as I kept on being sent down the line in the pecking order. Once the exercise was over and we had lined up according to height, there I was bang in the middle, Mr Average.

I work full-time and do my best in my spare time to serve God and remain active in my church. I do believe that I have a story to tell, a story of transformation and growth in faith. It is my hope that in reading my story, the average ordinary person in the Lord, (pretty much most of us) will be inspired to see just what God can do with an ordinary life.

For the Evangelists, those full-time ministers called by God to lead large movements and to have a significant impact in God's Kingdom, hopefully, this book will encourage and inspire you to continue to feed the flock, those ordinary people, the worker bees, who go out day after day and sow the seeds inspired by your writing and preaching.

To respect the privacy of certain individuals and to avoid re-opening old wounds for people whose relatives or friends may have been the victims in some of the cases referred to, I have changed certain names and locations. Everything else disclosed, is factual.

Prologue: The Evidence of God's Grace

"For God loved the world so much that he gave his one and only Son, so that everyone who believes in him will not perish but have eternal life". John 3:16 NLT

Before going through the compelling evidence supporting Christianity, as a starting point, I would like to declutter the path around the perception many people have concerning the character of God. Some believe that God is a despot, who will send those who refuse to fall into line, straight to a place of eternal destruction. Personally, I would not be very motivated to spend an eternity with such a God after my time of life on earth has concluded. If God were a despotic and harsh ruler, demanding worship and subjugation, I personally would bow out of the faith and accept my losses. I would be very grateful to God for granting me life but would take my punishment in the after-life rather than spend eternity with such a self-centred, all-powerful and all-knowing Creator.

Fortunately, the God I have come to know does not fit this description. Far from sending his created beings to a dreadful demise due to our failure to reach His standard of holiness, he has made a provision to save us from inevitable doom. I think about it like this. We are all drowning in a sea of iniquity. Our ship is sunk and it is only a matter of time before we can no longer tread water and succumb to the inevitable. Death will come to us all. God in His mercy has sent us a lifeboat. That lifeboat is analogous of Jesus. Jesus has plenty of space on board to save us all. It is our choice whether we swim like crazy and cling to him. The alternative is to stay put, keep our faith in ourselves or something else, and take our chances.

It is only when considering this wonderful act of grace, balancing it against the weight of sin and the pain and destruction sin brings into the world, that God's amazing love and compassion can begin to be fully understood and appreciated. Have you ever been sinned against? Have you ever struggled to forgive somebody who has hurt you? Forgiveness can be a hard thing to do. Now do the maths around God's forgiveness. Everyone, even good people, sin. Each sin hurts God and pollutes the world. Yet God forgives every sin of every person who accepts His son, Jesus, as his or her saviour, millions upon millions of people throughout history. That is a lot of power, and lot of forgiveness.

The world is a harsh place and in this world, we can get into a whole lot of trouble without doing anything wrong. Perhaps we made an honest error or were simply in the wrong place at the wrong time. In God's Kingdom, the opposite is the case. We can receive a whole lot of blessing without doing much right. Nothing can earn God's grace. We receive it out of mercy and loving-kindness. Now this type of character I can follow, and am motivated to want to spend an eternity with Him.

Most of us who have spent any length of time in the work force have experienced good bosses and bad bosses. I recall one Detective Inspector; I'll refer to him as DI Grey, who presided over me during my time as a Trainee Detective on CID. When I was posted to his department, I was looking forward to learning from someone who had a reputation for being meticulous and knowledgeable.

Nevertheless, my time under his supervision was not an enjoyable experience. Far from building me up and nurturing my confidence, he seemed to go to great lengths to expose my limitations and had an attitude of defending his own position at all costs. Many of his comments on our crime reports were negative, placing the Investigating Officers in a bad light. I found this very surprising, as these reports were relevant and disclosed to the defence.

I recall an amusing story that I cannot corroborate as true, but I believe to be so. It involved a *tough as old boots* Detective Sergeant from up north named Paul Welsh. DI Grey had been up to his usual custom of conducting a scathing review of a specific investigation Paul Welsh was supervising. On the narrative of the review, the DI appeared to suggest some degree of impropriety from the investigating officer. Paul Welsh was not one for being intimidated by rank and tended to stand his ground if he thought he was right. He closed the crime down and on the narrative of the report wrote words to the following effect:

This investigation is now untenable by virtue of the fact that the reviewing Detective Inspector would quite likely be called to court as a witness for the defence should this case go to trial.

Until recently I was unable to verify if this was true or not, as I never saw the report with my own eyes, I only offer hearsay evidence of this, however I knew Paul Welsh well enough to be confident he had it in him to adopt such an approach, and I have subsequently been able to confirm the accuracy on the episode. The fact that he was abruptly moved to my department shortly after, only served to heighten my suspicions. Coincidently, I recently spent some time with a former colleague from my days working in the Newham Command, Barry.

We were at the national Police Rehabilitation Centre in Goring, Oxfordshire. We were both receiving treatment for injuries. It turned out he was at the desk next to the Inspector's office when Detective Sergeant Paul Welsh turned the air in the office blue with profanity and stormed into DI Grey's office and threatened to throw him out of the window.

DS Welsh effectively ended his tenure as a Main Office Detective Sergeant with that outburst and was posted as my new 'Skipper' the very next day; tucked away on the old Robbery Team at Stratford. I remember when I heard about the retirement of DI Grey, thinking to myself what a waste of knowledge and ability. Perhaps he was a victim of circumstance after a case under his jurisdiction had gone badly wrong and the police were criticised at the IPCC review of the actions taken by investigating officers, causing the reputation of the Metropolitan Police Service to come into disrepute. Subsequently, DI Grey appeared to become so consumed with self-preservation that he was a hindrance to those of us who were up and coming, eager to grow and improve and deal with whatever investigations came our way. There is a lesson there on how being self-consumed at the expense of others can damage the legacy of even the most capable leaders.

Conversely, I have been supervised by Sergeants who showed me respect, offered me help and advice in some of the more difficult situations, even defending my corner when the heat was coming down from on high. DS Paul Welsh was like this.

You will not be surprised that I achieved some of my best results under such supervisors. The point here is that I happily worked hard under such Sergeants, wanting to reward their trust with due diligence and a high professional standard on my part. I worked hard for these leaders not out of fear, but out of loyalty, because of their attitude towards me.

God has demonstrated His love to a great extent through the death of His son, Jesus Christ. To all intents and purposes, Jesus was a sacrificial lamb to atone for our sins. For this reason, I find it easy to submit to God's standard and will for my life. I do not follow out of fear, as fear is not enough. If fear was the motivation, I think I would rebel. What compels me is Christ's love.

When Jesus was nailed to the cross, it is recorded in the gospels that He cried out "Father forgive them, they don't know what they do." (Luke 23:34) Even in the moment of his greatest pain and torture, Jesus (God in flesh) cried out for others, even his enemies. The very people that sent him to the cross and those who nailed him to it could do nothing to earn redemption. Jesus words and actions on that fateful day are what earned their redemption.

I mentioned earlier that in the world in which we live, we can get into a lot of trouble without doing an awful lot wrong. Something really brought this home to me early on in my career as a Substantive Detective. I was moved from the Central CID Office at Plaistow and was based on the Proactive Crime Unit in Stratford. I was posted to football duty for a West Ham United home game. Football games take a lot of policing and someone has to deal with those who are arrested and placed in Police custody. I was on duty when two men were arrested for being drunk and disorderly and, in their drunken state, decided they were not going to go quietly from the stadium. It took about six police officers to win the argument and force was used.

One of the arresting officers, (now a good friend of mine) was assaulted in the incident, sustaining superficial injuries. Assault on a police officer was added to the charge sheet. I interviewed both of them. This was a simple low-key case which was not one that I felt needed an excessive amount of my attention. I viewed the CCTV evidence, collected it, and the footage that captured the arrest, I exhibited as evidence. The footage that captured the crowd in the area where the two were seated, showed nothing of relevance so I consigned it to my *unused material* as it did not assist the defence or undermine the prosecution case. I collated the statements, presented the evidence to the CPS and the two accused were duly charged.

On the day of the trial, inexplicably the Crown lawyer decided to withdraw the case stating that she believed the police had used an excessive amount of force. This was a big shock to me. I viewed the footage of the incident several times and arrived at the same conclusion every time. It was a standard roll-around (Police speak for wrestling with suspects who were resisting arrest). My colleagues used the force that was necessitated by the resistance of the two drunken and rather hefty individuals in front of them. CS spray was used, but the circumstances justified the use of force.

Subsequently, with the case withdrawn, the two accused, lodged a complaint against the police. I was contacted by the Department of Professional Standards and informed that the Lawyers representing the two complainants had accused me of deliberately withholding CCTV evidence that would have exonerated their clients. I was asked to provide a statement detailing my actions and I duly complied. Of the many officers involved in the case, I was the only one who was not formally interviewed by the DPS, and I think this must have lulled me into a false sense of security.

What transpired during the DPS investigation was that I had not handled the unused CCTV according to protocol. What I should have done was inform the CPS on my schedule of unused material that I also had CCTV from a camera pointing at the crowd, which did not contain any relevant footage. In my naïve logic as a newly promoted Detective, the footage had no relevance so I had no need to disclose it.

This was an error on my part born out of inexperience in how to handle unused material, certainly not dishonesty in a misguided attempt to cover up an impropriety. What the lawyers representing the accused argued was that, the fact the unused CCTV did not show any trouble was proof that the police had acted wrongfully in arresting the two men in the first place.

About eighteen months after the investigation had begun, all police officers being investigated, myself included, received notification from the investigating Sergeant that the case had been sent to the CPS, and the reviewing lawyer had decided that no charges should be made against any officer concerned. I scrolled down to my own name. My heart sank in surprise when I saw that on the report was an accusation of, attempting to pervert the course of justice. (If convicted this comes with a seven-year prison sentence!) It was marked *No Further Action, due to insufficient evidence.* I was put out by this. What I would have loved to have seen was 'no case to answer.' However, my administrative error in how I handled the unused CCTV was sufficient cause to arouse suspicion. It dawned on me for first time when I read through the closing report that I was almost in a whole lot of trouble without doing anything morally wrong.

> My heart sank in surprise when I saw that on the report was an accusation of attempting to pervert the course of justice.

Conversely, with God, we as a collective have done a whole lot of wrong. Our rage, our pride, our dishonesty, our propensity towards selfishness, which often hurts others, all conspires to build a case against us. However, in Jesus, we have the ultimate double jeopardy defence. He has already *served the time* for our crimes. Therefore, no charges can stand up against us when our accuser lists them before God's judgment seat. The answer for every crime accusation for every soul is the same: Jesus has paid the price. Theologically this is God's perfect system of justice. Just as through one man, Adam, sin came into the world and placed us all under a sentence of death. Through one man, Jesus, who led a perfect and blameless life, the sentence of death was transformed into a gracious pardon.

One of my best memories of my time working in Newham was when I reported to DS Paul Welsh. We were very different characters. On the one hand, Paul was no stranger to profanity. When the mood set in, literally every other word would have activated the proverbial *bleep* machine. Sometimes this would be triggered by some perceived incompetence.

On the other hand, I was the Christian, perhaps in the eyes of some a 'southern softie'. When we were posted together, I am sure a few of our colleagues wondered how this working relationship was going to pan out, as it was a potential culture clash. However, before Paul and I worked on the same team, we had already discovered some common ground, sharing gym time together, pumping weights.

I remember one occasion in particular at Forest Gate Police Station. Paul was training with typically heavy weights, bench-pressing without a spotter, using the Olympic bar. Suddenly crash! Somehow, he ended up on the floor with the Olympic bar millimetres from his forehead. We were the only two using the gym at the time. I thought I had just witnessed a tragic life ending accident. I rushed over to him my heart still pumping, and lifted the bar away from him. Paul got up and took a moment to compose himself, then casually resumed his workout as though nothing had happened.

Surprisingly we struck up some good *faith* conversations during our late turn shifts when we had a bit of down time. Another amusing anecdote from my time working with DS Paul Welsh is when I was transferred to another unit and my period working under Paul's supervision was coming to an end, Paul piped up in his gruff northerner accent, "*Randal, we are both failures. You are a failure because you have failed to turn me to God. On the other hand, I am a failure because I have failed to make you swear!*"

> **You are a failure because you have failed to turn me to God.**

Since concluding the prologue to part one, I have been in contact with Paul Welsh who read the relevant narrative above. He responded by providing me with the following short statement:

> I've read your extracts about DS Paul Welsh with a smile on my face.
>
> Time has diminished my memory on the events you outline but I can confirm that they occurred along the lines you have recounted.
>
> My only concern is about the entry on the crime report. I remember the investigation but not the finer details. I would not have closed the enquiry down because further investigation was required. I believe my point was that

DI Grey's continued supervision of the enquiry was untenable as he was effectively alleging misconduct and the crime report was not the place to document that enquiry. In fact, I went further and had the crime reallocated to a new team.

My favourite recollection of our conversations is when you told me you and your wife had fallen out and not speaking. When I asked why you informed me, in a very serious tone, that it was a disagreement about the interpretation of a point in the Bible. For once, I was speechless.

Happy times

Paul

Note from the author; Concerning the alleged falling out with Mrs Porter which was alluded to at the end of former Detective Sergeant Paul Welsh's statement, I choose to make no comment!

Chapter One

Historical Jesus

The best place to begin the story of my grounds for conviction is with the *person* of Jesus. Some may argue that Jesus is a legend. At this juncture, it is appropriate that I present some of the evidence I considered when taking the decision to follow the Christian faith.

Something that really grabbed my attention early on was that there is overwhelming proof that Jesus was a real historical person who lived in first century Israel.

Most people in their minds eye have two cabinets for storing the information they receive. The truth cabinet and the fiction cabinet. What people have a tendency to do with the Bible is create another storage section, a Biblical truth file. This can be faith diluting because it does the job of relegating Biblical truth to a lesser truth than those truths stored in the Truth file. I can tell you now that you should chuck the Biblical truth file away and merge the information with that contained in the Truth cabinet. The historicity of Jesus is irrefutable and I do not believe that any sensible argument can be constructed, denying that Jesus Christ, the Carpenter and Teacher from Nazareth, is a real historical figure. Julius Caesar, King Henry VIII, Napoleon Bonaparte, Adolf Hitler, Winston Churchill and Jesus Christ are all historical figures. The relevant question about Jesus is not did he exist? But who was he really? I will explore this question later.

Another very good question to ask is; Other than the Bible what evidence is there that Jesus really lived? There is plenty of evidence about Jesus, the historical person outside of the Bible. So, the Bible is not our only source of information about Jesus. His existence can be corroborated by non-Christian sources too. The first information I came across external to the Bible was details of a letter written by a

Roman Governor. The letter was written by Plinius Secondus, to the Roman Emperor Trajan. He was seeking advice on an important social problem in his province. He had been authorising the killing of Christians at such a rate that he questioned whether it was wise to continue to do so. Not just adults but children were also being killed. Should he kill all who professed the Christian faith or just some? In the same letter, he gives mention to Christ "whom they affirmed as a god."

The letter also gives a pretty clear insight into the plight of the Christ followers. They were made to bow before a statue of Trajan and affirm him as a god, or die. What startled Plinius was that in his experience, the followers of the Christ God would choose death rather than worship the emperor. This places a whole new meaning to the affirmation that I said on the day of my baptism.

> The followers of the Christ God would choose death rather than Emperor worship.

There are two questions we are asked immediately prior to baptism. The first is; do you believe that Jesus Christ is the son of God? The second is; what is your good confession? My own answer to the second question was the same answer I have heard at all the baptisms I have attended: "Jesus is Lord." For the first century Christians under Trajan to say Jesus is Lord was a potential death sentence.

A point to ponder is that these were Roman subjects being executed. They were members of the most advanced empire the world had seen, and were educated sensible people, not ignorant tribal nomads. They were prepared to die for a reason. They knew that all the stories circulating about Jesus and the resurrection were coming from eyewitnesses. In a court of law, an eyewitness account carries a lot of weight. The evidence of several eyewitnesses makes a case even stronger to the point of being beyond a reasonable doubt.

If the number of eyewitnesses all saying the same thing are so numerous, the Counsel for the defence would no doubt instruct their client, the Accused, to present a guilty plea at the earliest opportunity at Court. In the first century, there were hundreds of eyewitnesses to the miracles of Jesus who were still living. Remember Jesus often preached to large crowds and some of the healing miracles occurred in front of a multitude. Word of the two miracles of Jesus producing food out of thin air, feeding the crowd of thousands with a couple of fish and a few loaves of bread would have spread like a wild fire as so many benefitted from these supernatural feedings. (Matthew 14:13 & 15:29).

But how do we know that the whole Jesus-rising-from-the-dead thing, is not just a made up story? What about the conspiracy theory, could the followers of Jesus have stolen the body from the tomb and spread the rumour that Jesus had risen from the dead?

It is not as easy to spread and perpetuate a lie of this magnitude as you might think. For example, let us consider Margaret Thatcher. She was the first female Prime Minister of Great Britain and came to power when I was a teenager. When I had grown up with two sons, she was still in power. Imagine if someone on social media had posted a claim that after a cabinet meeting Mrs Thatcher had missed her train and decided to walk on water across the River Thames. I would soon shout this ludicrous claim down. I was living at the time of the Thatcher Administration and such an incredible occurrence would surely have been captured on camera by one of the many tourists in Westminster, and made headline news.

True there was no social media in first century Israel; their version would have been through public proclamation at market places and Town centres; like the old English Town Crier.

The reason the Christians under the rule of Trajan were not prepared to curse Christ and worship Trajan as god, was that they were highly confident beyond reasonable doubt, that the reports about Jesus were true. No one could deny the testimony of the miracles Jesus performed because the Middle Eastern markets and town centres, as well as those of other corners of the Roman Empire were too full of witnesses to the miracles.

Under Roman rule, there was a period of around two hundred years of relative calm and peace. This period is referred to in history books as the *Pax Romana*. During the *Pax Romana*, the various provinces swallowed by the Roman Empire became linked to each other by an infra structure of roads, facilitating travel between provinces. Truly God works out times and places and the timing of Jesus coming at what was at the time the most advanced the world had ever been in terms of road networks, enabled the Good news of great miracles to be spread by eyewitnesses. This is the reason that the four accounts of the life and ministry of Jesus, known as the Gospels, once written, survived not only the first century, but the course of time.

The Plinius Secondus letter is just one important bit of evidence referencing the historical credentials of Jesus Christ. Further evidence can be gleaned from one of the eminent Jewish historians of the first century Flavius Josephus, born 37 AD, just a few years after the death of Jesus. Josephus was not a Christian; he was a Jew and commander of the Jewish forces in Galilee. He writes with some depth in his historical account <u>The Antiquities of the Jews</u>, about the person of Jesus.

It is important to note that he was neither pro-Jesus or impartial. In fact, it would be safe to say he would have been anti-Jesus. Like the majority of Jews in his time, he looked elsewhere for the Messiah and it is generally accepted that Josephus considered the Roman Emperor Vespasian (renowned for military success) to be Israel's Messiah. In his work <u>The Wars of The Jews</u>, Josephus wrote that Vespasian fulfilled the messianic oracles. <u>The Antiquities of The Jews</u> is another important historical work. It is a twenty-volume documented account of the history of Israel. The most significant section of the *Antiquities* known as the *Testimonium Flavianum*, actually caused me raised eyebrows of surprise when I first read it.

> "Now there was about this time Jesus, a wise man, if it be lawful to call him a man, for he was a doer of wonderful works, a teacher of such men as receive the truth with pleasure. He drew over to him both many of the Jews, and many of the Gentiles. He was the Christ; and when Pilate, at the suggestion of the principal men amongst us, had condemned him to the cross, those that loved him at the first did not forsake him, for he appeared to them alive again the third day, as the divine prophets had foretold these and ten thousand other wonderful things concerning him; and the tribe of Christians, so named from him, are not extinct to this day." Antiquities 18.3.3.

Sceptics argue that this testimony from a Jewish historian in the employ of Rome is just too good to be true. I concede that they may be right. Why would Josephus leave himself open to the accusation of treason and punishment by execution by writing such a proclamation of Jesus 'messiahship', in a work sponsored by Rome?

The Roman hierarchy was extremely sensitive to the concept of a Jewish Messiah overthrowing Roman rule in Israel, and the possibly domino effect this could have in their other conquered provinces. It is a strong possibility that the wording of Josephus was paraphrased by a later Christian copyist. However, my point here is that through Josephus's work, The Antiquities of The Jews, the *Encyclopaedia Britannica* of the day in relation to Jewish history, we have extra-biblical evidence that the person Jesus is historical. I concede that the Josephus references to Jesus messianic credentials are spurious because of the possibility that they have been tinkered with, making the reference questionable. However, my point in introducing Josephus in support of the case for Jesus Christ's historicity is that, through Josephus's *Antiquities,* the world has extra-biblical evidence that the person, Jesus, is historical.

It is generally the accepted view that Josephus did indeed write about Him. Therefore, we have to conclude, that in the first century, it was accepted as a fact that there was a teacher (rabbi) named Jesus who had a large following, and was crucified. It is only what Josephus actually wrote about Jesus that is questioned.

Having established that the person of Jesus is factual and historical, we then need to formulate our opinion on what He said and believed. Jesus was very clear in His teaching that He was the chosen one, the very Messiah all of Israel had been waiting for since their days of captivity in Egypt. There are three possibilities: the liar, lunatic and lord postulation.

If Jesus knew he was not the Messiah but claimed that He was, He was simply a liar. The problem with the liar postulation is the lack of motive. Jesus knew very well that if He continued with the teaching pathway He had adopted, He would evoke the wrath of the authorities. Indeed, in our examination of the gospels we can see that Jesus predicted His death at the hands of the establishment. (Luke 9:22).

The second postulation is that Jesus was not the Messiah but believed that he was. If this postulation is correct, then Jesus was completely delusional. The problem with this theory is that a close examination of Jesus' teachings, especially the parables shows the considered opinions of a very balanced individual. Most certainly his words were not the rants of a mad person.

The only other option left for us, if we dismiss the first two, is that what Jesus believed and taught was in fact true. If this is the case then Jesus, by definition, was indeed Lord! If Jesus was Lord then, he certainly is Lord now and will continue to be so in the future. That means if we accept the reality of Jesus being who he said he was, we are called to make a decision on how we should respond.

Chapter Two

A Smoking Gun

When all this comes true - and surely it will then they will know that a prophet has been among them. (Ezekiel 33:33)

The book of Daniel is a remarkable chronicle of history. What makes this history book so different however is that it has chronicled the history in advance! For a few years now, I have been part of a teaching group in the East London Church of Christ. Once a year the team embarks on a project, whereby we take a book of the Bible in isolation, study it and produce a commentary in the form of a month-long quiet time series. We carve up the book into sections, for which each member takes personal responsibility.

Once we have peer reviewed each other's work, Simon Dixon, who leads the group, then produces the completed document for distribution amongst the congregation. A couple of years ago we gained a new addition to the group, Martin, who assisted greatly with our production of a Quiet Time series on the Old Testament Book of Daniel.

During one of our progress meetings Martin commented that the prophecies of Daniel were so accurate that we have, in scripture, a *smoking gun of evidence* as far as biblical apologetics is concerned. In this chapter, I will explain why.

I am convinced that the major part of the prophecies in the book of Daniel are to do with the fourth empire predicted in chapter two, that of Rome. This makes good sense because Rome was the reigning power when Jesus and his church were introduced into the world. Rome was the power that presided over the crucifixion of Jesus. This was the power that attempted to eradicate the church when the 11th Emperor of Rome, Domitian, was ruling. In order to grasp the intricacies of the detailed revelations in the book of Daniel, it is necessary to have an understanding of the history of the Roman Empire and its paralleled interactions with the church of Christ.

I will not be discussing the prophecies relating to the Roman Empire. One of the reasons for this is that some of the theories about the prophecies of Daniel and their fulfilment are subjective and open to interpretation. For this reason, I am sticking with the non-subjective part of the Daniel prophesy which was spelled out in chapter eight covering the rise and fall of Greece and the fate of its first King. I will focus my discussion on this area of prophesy. Below is the verse from chapter eight, which spells out whom the prophecy is about.

> "The shaggy goat is the king of Greece and the large horn between his eyes the first king. The four horns that replaced the one that was broken represent four kingdoms that will emerge from his nation but will not have his same power." Daniel 8:21-22

As a starting point, I will give some background information before I take a quick tour of the book, this will be a useful refresher for those familiar with the book and induction for those not so familiar.

The book of Daniel was probably completed around 530 BC, most likely after the capture of Babylon by Cyrus. Israel had previously been defeated by the Invading Babylonian armies, Jerusalem had been sacked and the most prominent individuals, essentially young healthy men with an aptitude for learning, were selected to be assimilated into Babylonian society with their new masters. Daniel and three other young men with whom he formed a close friendship were amongst those exiled to Babylon.

Chapter one.

Daniel is renamed Belteshazzar, and his friends were stripped of their identities and renamed Shadrach, Meshach and Abednego. They take an early stand, declining to eat the rich royal food opting instead for a strict vegetarian diet. This act of defiance in itself causes their Governor a great deal of anxiety. However, his fears are abated when all four men appear healthier than their peers.

Chapter two.

Nebuchadnezzar has a dream, which he keeps secret and asks his chief wise men to interpret for him. Unable to do so, the king responds to their failure by issuing a harsh despotic decree sentencing all the wise men to death. Daniel saves the day when he tactfully speaks to the bearer of the bad news and requests an audience with the king. He then tells the king exactly what he dreamed and then interprets the dream as well.

Chapter three.

The Babylonian king, Nebuchadnezzar, constructs a huge golden monument and issues a decree that whenever the royal music plays everyone should bow and worship the image. Daniel's friends refuse to do this and their insubordination leads to them all being sentenced to execution by being thrown into a fiery furnace. So enraged is the king at the humiliating refusal of these subordinates to yield to his demands, he has the furnace stoked, seven times hotter than usual; so hot that his own soldiers are killed during the process of taking the three activists to the furnace. An Angel visits them whilst they are inside and to the astonishment of the king all three survive without even the smell of burning or even a singed hair on their heads.

Chapter four.

Nebuchadnezzar has another dream this time about a tree. Daniel is again able to give the king an interpretation. The dream is bad news for the king as the interpretive meaning is that king Nebuchadnezzar will lose his mind and go insane. Twelve months later this comes to pass and the once noble king is reduced to living a hermit's life in the wild and eating grass like cattle. The insanity is temporary, and after a period in exile, the king is restored to sound mind and resumes his role as the reigning monarch.

Chapter five.

Fast forward to the reign of a new king, Belshazzar who was the son and viceroy of Nabonidus. The puppet king throws a huge banquet for a thousand nobles. He orders that the treasured cups seized from the temple in Jerusalem, be bought so that he and his guests can celebrate in style. Out of the blue, something supernatural occurs when the fingers from a human hand writes some words in the plaster of the wall in the banqueting hall. The message is in a language the king does not understand and it is reliable Daniel who accomplishes the task of revealing to the king the mystery of the writing on the wall. It is bad news as it spells the end to Belshazzar's reign and that very night he is assassinated. For Belshazzar, the writing was most definitely on the wall!

Chapter six.

A new king, Darius, is in power and he delegates the running of his affairs to a hundred and twenty designated personnel. Daniel is amongst this number and distinguishes himself above all the others. Possibly fuelled by jealousy, a peer group conducts an audit on Daniel's work hoping to expose some negligence or dishonesty. To their dismay, they find no fault in his administration of government affairs so they plot to trap him over some issue of his faith.

Knowing that he prays regularly to the God of the conquered Israelites, they dupe the king into issuing a decree making it illegal to pray to any god or man during a one-month period. Only the king can be prayed to. The king agrees. The edict is issued and Daniel, on hearing of the royal edict, goes straight home and prays to the God of Israel. The conspirators expose Daniel's defiance to the king who reluctantly orders that Daniel is thrown into the lions' den.

Miraculously, Daniel survives his ordeal unscathed. He is released from the den and the conspirators who set the trap receive from King Darius, 'their just desserts,' for conspiring to force his hand to execute Daniel a respected and trusted administrator, his most competent and trustworthy official. They were all, along with families, thrown to the lions, meeting a horrific end.

Chapter seven.

Daniel dreams of four beasts. A lion, a bear, a leopard and a terrifying and frightening beast, the like of which have never been seen before and cannot be named. Troubled by the dream Daniel approaches a man who interprets that the four beasts are representative of four future kingdoms, the fourth of which will be the worst of all.

Chapter eight.

About two years later, Daniel has a vision of a ram and a goat. An angel interprets the dream for him. The rampaging and unstoppable ram, which menacingly rules the world, meets a sudden and violent demise when a goat with a prominent horn appears from the west and charges at the ram, defeating it easily. The goat becomes great but at the height of its power, the great horn is broken. The angel Gabriel tells Daniel what the dream means explaining that the ram represents the Medo-Persian Empire and the goat the Greek empire, the great horn being the first king of that empire.

Chapter nine.

Daniel prays. He confesses his own sin and the corporate sins of all Israelites in turning away from their God. Gabriel visits Daniel again. He gives Daniel some prophetic time frames that appear to be a period when the transgressions of the people will be allowed to continue until the coming of the anointed one and his subsequent cutting off. This appears to be a clear messianic prophecy predicting the crucifixion of Jesus Christ.

Chapter ten.

Daniel sees a vision of a man. This event takes place in the third year of the reign of a new king, Cyrus. The vision is of an angel who reassures Daniel that his prayers have been heard and that he (the angel) has been sent in response. From what the angel discloses, it can be gleaned that there is a supernatural battle, which is shaping world events.

Chapter eleven.

Future events and kings are spoken of; one king in particular will rise and exalt himself. (There is a very strong argument that this self-exalting one was Domitian the 11th Emperor of Rome.)

Chapter twelve is apocalyptic and speaks of the resurrection of the dead and end times.

Most people are familiar with the narrative of the first six chapters, which incorporate the account of Daniel's friends being thrown into the fiery furnace, also the account of Daniel being thrown to the lions who decided to fast for the night enabling Daniel to survive his ordeal.

From chapter seven onwards, the book of Daniel becomes much harder to understand. By way of explanation, the beasts described in chapter seven can be linked with the vision of Daniel in chapter two. The identity of each world power has been debated for centuries and interpretations vary. Popular opinion suggests the following:

Head of gold / lion; Babylonia, present day Iraq. Once mighty enough to rule over nations, defeating the Assyrian Empire, Babylon was the major world power during the lifetime of Daniel, but was the shortest reigning of the four mighty empires, only enjoying supremacy between 626 BC – 539 BC when defeated by Medo-Persia, a mere hundred and thirteen years of world domination.

Chest and arms of silver / bear; Medo–Persian; Western Asia which, at its greatest extent included all of the territory of modern-day Iran, Turkey, Kuwait, Syria, Jordan, Israel, Palestine, Lebanon and Afghanistan. The Medo-Persian Empire came to prominence in 539 BC and reigned supreme until the armies of Alexander the Great swept all away all before it around 330 BC A period of two hundred and thirteen years of world domination.

Belly and thighs of bronze / leopard; Greece. The ancient Greek Empire with Alexander the Great as its driving force assimilated much of the known world and influenced every society that followed with its knowledge, customs, writings and laws, including the Roman Empire. Koine Greek became the common language of the people. Greece was the supreme world power for the period up until the mightiest of all empires that of Rome, who took over the world from 63 BC A period of two hundred and sixty-seven years.

Legs of iron / terrifying and frightening beast; Roman Empire, the dominant world force when Jesus was sent into the human race via the nation of Israel through the virgin, Mary, a direct descendent of Israel's second king, David. Truly, the mighty Roman army was a terrifying unstoppable beast, which conquered all before it on the field of battle. Rome ruled as a world super-power for the better part of a millennium.

The writings that make up the book of Daniel are most likely a collation of Daniel's memoirs, edited together, by an associate after his death. I have assumed this position based on the style of writing, the narrative of Daniel is written in the third person. If Daniel himself had put the book together, I would imagine the narrative would be in the first-person. The collation of the prophetic book was possibly completed after Cyrus sacked Babylon in 539 BC. The Greek Empire under Alexander the Great came to prominence in 330 BC almost two centuries later.

So just to make it clear what I am saying is that chapter eight of the book of Daniel wrote world history in advance. If this is a true statement, then it logically follows that Daniel's prophetic dreams and visions were of supernatural origin, the most likely source being God Himself.

Shortly I will discuss some circumstances that make it very clear that chapter eight of Daniel prophesied history in a very detailed way.

Firstly a little about the language used in the narrative. Daniel dreams of beasts, which are an analogy of world empires, spread over time. When you think about it, the European Union started off as a trading co-operative but evolved into a different type of organisation that devoured previously independent nations, setting laws of government, even developing its own flag. The fledgling trading co-operative evolved into a European Union of member states, centrally governed. The freedom of movement so sought after by the European Commission, is an old tool adopted by previous empirical powers from Babylon through to Rome.

The United Kingdom for example was once made up of warring factions, Saxons and Celts and Clans in Scotland and Ireland. It is now a much different "beast" unified under the Union Jack. This very beast would be split into two if the Scottish First Minister, Nicola Sturgeon, has her way and presents Scotland with a post Brexit referendum. When you read of beasts, think empires that like a beast of the field, is conceived, born, grows, develops and eventually dies. Do not let all this talk of beasts distract you too much.

Now, we need to consider Daniel 8:1-3;

> In the third year of King Belshazzar's reign, I, Daniel, had a vision, after the one that had already appeared to me. ² In my vision I saw myself in the citadel of Susa in the province of Elam; in the vision I was beside the Ulai Canal. ³ I looked up, and there before me was a ram with two horns, standing beside the canal, and the horns were long. One of the horns was longer than the other but grew up later.

The passage refers to two horns. In apocalyptic language, horns are usually analogous of kings or national powers. The ram being referred to, is the Medo-Persian dual empire, so the two horns are the two kings or national powers of the dual empire. The next statement *"one of the horns was longer that the other but grew up later."* History was to reveal that the two strands of the Medo-Persian Empire grew at different rates. The Medes initially being the more prominent but Persia later became very much, the senior partner. Initially Persia was a province within the Median Empire. However, under the rule of Cyrus the Great, Persia took the lead in establishing the Medo-Persian Empire.

Daniel 8:4:

> "I watched the ram as he charged towards the West and the North and the South. No animal could stand against him, and none could rescue from his power. He did as he pleased and became great."

The military conquests of the Medo-Persians were actually in sequence with this Daniel prophesy. Babylon to the West was conquered, Lydia to the North, Egypt to the South. The exact same order of conquest as detailed in Daniel 8:4.

Now take a look at Daniel 8:5:

> "As I was thinking about this, suddenly a goat with a prominent horn between his eyes came from the West, crossing the whole earth without touching the ground."

The goat we know is the Greek empire under Alexander the Great. Firstly, we know for a fact that the Greeks usurped the Medo-Persians as the next world power. This is how history panned out. Secondly, later in verse 21, Daniel is given a revelation that the Goat is symbolic of Greece. Hence there is no argument around the fulfilment of this prophesy. For two hundred years this was simply a prophesy. Then it happened and became a fulfilment of biblical prophecy.

Now look at Daniel 8:8:

"The goat became very great, but at the height of his power his horn was broken off."

Who do you think the passage could be referring to here? The military leader behind the expansion of the Greek Empire was of course, Alexander the Great. What made him great?

Firstly, in the results-orientated business of waging war, he literally conquered all that was before him. There has been the story in circulation, from antiquity, of King Alexander weeping, as there were no more lands to be conquered. Even conquering the known world did not bring happiness and anti-climax followed his great achievements. Over a twelve-year period, his armies were victorious in one campaign after another. Secondly, it could be said he was a born leader being the son of King Philip of Macedon, itself a warring nation.

Thirdly, Alexander the Great was educated at the very highest level. His teacher was arguably the greatest intellect of his time, Aristotle. There is simply no doubt that like the goat in the vision of Daniel 8, Alexander became great. After the destruction of the remaining Medo-Persian strongholds, the final one being the City of Tyre, Alexander took Palestine and headed towards Jerusalem.

The Jews decided to appease rather than fight. Appeasement was always a tactical option when a large army was headed towards you. The learned delegation sent to Alexander pointed out to him that their scriptures had prophesied his victories. Indeed, if we are to accept the words of the historian, Josephus, they used the book of Daniel. This is what Josephus wrote;

"And when the book of Daniel was showed to him, in which Daniel declared that one of the Greeks should destroy the empire of the Persians he supposed that he himself was the person intended; and as he was then glad, he ….asked them what favours they wanted of him. The high priest requested that they …might pay no tribute on the seventh year. He granted all they desired."

Now consider Daniel 8:8b:

> "And in its place four prominent horns grew up towards the four winds of heaven."

At the time of writing, this would not have made any sense. However, as history has now panned out, we know what happened after Alexander's conquest around the known world. The horn broke, (Alexander died) suddenly, whilst still young and at the height of his power. Alexander had no suitable heir to his kingdom as his wife, Roxanna, was still carrying his child. What happened next is that four of his generals carved up his empire between them. Could these be the four prominent horns?

Certainly, the book of Daniel got the circumstances right, it even got the number of successors right. Again, now that history has played out we can name the four horns of Daniel 8:8. Antigonus ruled the East territory from Syria to India. Cassander ruled the West Macedonia and Greece, Lysimachus the North Asia Minor and Ptolemy South Egypt and Palestine.

Daniel 8:22:

> "But will not have the same power."

The sum of the four horns, (kingships / kingdoms) that Alexander the Great's empire was divided into never did match up to the sum of the whole under his kingship. Indeed, within a relatively short period the generals were fighting amongst themselves.

> **The fulfilled prophesies contained in the book of Daniel are so precise that they are indeed tantamount to a smoking gun**

The fulfilled prophesies contained in the book of Daniel are so precise that they are indeed tantamount to a *smoking gun* in terms of evidence that the source of the information is supernatural; the Word of God rather than the word of man.

Daniel was merely the conduit through whom these revelations were given.

Sceptics have tried to assert that the book of Daniel is a hoax and that the book was written as late as 160BC, well after the events. Sceptics are forced into this supposition because the only alternative is to accept that the book is genuine and, as such, inspired by God. An interesting point to note is that the book of Daniel was accepted as scripture and sacred in the first century. Furthermore, there are fragments of the book of Daniel in the archaeological find of the last century, the Dead Sea Scrolls.

Therefore, in terms of textual criticism (covered in chapter 5) we have good reason to have confidence in the book of Daniel as the Essenes (The sect who maintained the library of Scrolls found at Qumran in the caves) had already accepted Daniel, as an important book. Clearly, they held copies offering some degree of extra-biblical attestation.

Chapter Three

Corroborative Evidence

Five years into my police service, I crossed over from uniform to suit; from a Police Constable to a trainee Detective Constable. During my training, I spent a couple of years based at Stratford Police Station on the Proactive Crime Unit. Whilst posted on the Burglary Robbery Squad, I was handed a case of an aggravated burglary.

A burglary is *aggravated*, when a weapon is taken into a house and a person inside is assaulted. This was the most serious case I had investigated in my career so far. A couple of things stood out for me in this investigation that makes it so memorable for me. Firstly, it was one of the few times that I can remember a victim of a crime attending the police station to thank me for the work I had done after the investigation was complete. I have been thanked before, and one victim even wrote a letter of thanks. But this was the only experience I have had of a victim turning up at the station unannounced, especially to thank me and say goodbye. Secondly, it was a real eye opener for me of the importance of corroborative evidence needed to prove a case and achieve a conviction in a court of law.

In this case, I had three victims who were assaulted and traumatised by the incident. Although injuries sustained were not serious, the psychological damage certainly was. In this sense, it was a life changing experience for them. All three victims decided to return to Poland afterwards. The victims were a male and female couple and the young man's sister who were all living together in a flat in Forest Gate. They were typically very hard working Eastern Europeans. From the fruits of their labour, they had purchased laptops, smart phones and other electronic gadgets.

One evening whilst relaxing at home a group of six men, wearing balaclavas and carrying an assortment of weapons forced their way into the flat, bound and gagged them whilst demanding money and bankcards with PIN numbers. The young man in particular was targeted and he thought he was going to be killed.

I took over the investigation and from the house arranged for a Crime Scene Examiner to take finger prints. About a week later, bingo!

He was so scared that he managed to escape by jumping out of the first-floor window, running onto the street to alert a neighbour who called the police. His escape prompted the gang to flee from the scene. I took over the investigation and arranged for a Crime Scene Examiner to take fingerprints from the house. About a week later, bingo! One of the prints came back with a trace.

I now had a name and, from police records, a photograph of the suspect whose fingerprint was found on a table in the flat. After a bit of a manhunt, which involved placing an advert in a Polish newspaper, my Polish suspect was arrested and I interviewed him. He offered no defence or explanation as to how his fingerprint came to be found on a table in the flat and exercised his right to decline answering any questions. I *bailed* him to return another day confident that once I had completed my enquiries I would have enough evidence to gain authority to charge him with aggravated burglary. I was wrong!

In those days, we had a Crown Prosecution lawyer based at the police station with whom we sat down and talked through the evidence. My appointment with the lawyer did not go very well. I was told that, as the table upon which the suspect's fingerprint had been found was a moveable object, the defence could argue that the print was already on the table when it was brought into the house. It would be difficult to prove beyond reasonable doubt that my suspect was involved in the burglary since none of the victims would be able to make an identification. I was facing the prospect of my suspect going free. This was eating away at me. I was unsettled by the prospect of being unable to obtain justice for my victims.

However, I did some further research on the police intranet concerning my suspect and realised in my investigation I had missed something. My suspect, on the same day as the offence, had been arrested within half an hour of the crime I was investigating. It got even better. He was arrested in close-proximity to the crime scene for my investigation. So not only did I have his fingerprint on an object inside the flat, I could place him nearby, literally around the corner within half an hour of the offence taking place. I took this new information to the Crown Prosecution Service and they authorised the charge. Corroboration was the key to success and made all the difference. The accused later pleaded guilty in Court and received a lengthy custodial sentence.

If we now apply the same importance of corroboration to the Bible, I would expect any incident written about Bible that can be verified by extra-biblical sources, to carry a lot of weight and add great value to the credibility of the event chronicled.

It is at this juncture that I would like to *camp out* around the 'darkness' that came over the land when Jesus was crucified. This event is attached to arguably the most important event in the Christian faith, the crucifixion. Can this mysterious darkening over the land on that day be corroborated? Let us take another look at the event, as detailed in the synoptic Gospels:

The Gospel according to Matthew 27:

> [45] *From noon until three in the afternoon darkness came over all the land.* [46] *About three in the afternoon Jesus cried out in a loud voice, 'Eli, Eli, lema sabachthani?' (which means 'My God, my God, why have you forsaken me?')*
>
> [47] *When some of those standing there heard this, they said, 'He's calling Elijah.'*
>
> [48] *Immediately one of them ran and got a sponge. He filled it with wine vinegar, put it on a staff, and offered it to Jesus to drink.* [49] *The rest said, 'Now leave him alone. Let's see if Elijah comes to save him.'*
>
> [50] *And when Jesus had cried out again in a loud voice, he gave up his spirit.*

The Gospel according to Mark 15:

> ³³ At noon, darkness came over the whole land until three in the afternoon. ³⁴ And at three in the afternoon Jesus cried out in a loud voice, 'Eloi, Eloi, lema sabachthani?' (which means 'My God, my God, why have you forsaken me?').
>
> ³⁵ When some of those standing near heard this, they said, 'Listen, he's calling Elijah.'
>
> ³⁶ Someone ran, filled a sponge with wine vinegar, put it on a staff, and offered it to Jesus to drink. 'Now leave him alone. Let's see if Elijah comes to take him down,' he said.
>
> ³⁷ With a loud cry, Jesus breathed his last.

The Gospel according to Luke 23:

> ⁴⁴ It was now about noon, and darkness came over the whole land until three in the afternoon, ⁴⁵ for the sun stopped shining. And the curtain of the temple was torn in two. ⁴⁶ Jesus called out with a loud voice, 'Father, into your hands I commit my spirit.' When he had said this, he breathed his last.
>
> ⁴⁷ The centurion, seeing what had happened, praised God and said, 'Surely this was a righteous man.' ⁴⁸ When all the people who had gathered to witness this sight saw what took place, they beat their breasts and went away. ⁴⁹ But all those who knew him, including the women who had followed him from Galilee, stood at a distance, watching these things.

So, the three synoptic gospels are all in agreement that there was a darkness that came over the land. Three different writers bear witness to the event. But, are there any sources external to the Bible? Can this incident, documented by the writers of the gospels, be corroborated?

The answer is a firm, yes. I will rely on evidence from the ancient historian Sextus Julius Africanus. Firstly, a little about who he was. It is suggested that he was a philosopher. Africanus travelled to Greece and Rome and went to Alexandria to study. Alexandria was a major city and economic centre in Egypt. He was attracted there by the fame of its catechetical school (relating to religious instruction), possibly about the year 215 AD. He knew Greek (in which language he wrote), Latin, and

Hebrew.

He was at one time a soldier and had been a pagan. It is believed that he converted to Christianity and that his works were written as a Christian. The fact that he spoke three languages is perhaps a positive indicator of to the calibre of the man. Africanus is introduced as evidential by Christian apologists, by virtue of the fact he was a historian who reported historical facts. Around 221 AD, he composed a comprehensive five-volume history of the world. He was also entrusted with the official responsibility of building the Emperor's library at the Pantheon in Rome.

Africanus writes the following:

> "On the whole world there pressed a most fearful darkness; and the rocks were rent by an earthquake, and many places in Judea and other districts were thrown down."
>
> This darkness, Thallus, in the third book of his History, calls, as appears to me without reason, an eclipse of the sun. For the Hebrews celebrate the Passover on the 14th day according to the moon, and the passion of our Saviour falls on the day before the Passover; but an eclipse of the sun takes place only when the moon comes under the sun. And it cannot happen at any other time but in the interval between the first day of the new moon and the last of the old, that is, at their junction: how then should an eclipse be supposed to happen when the moon is almost diametrically opposite the sun? Let opinion pass however; let it carry the majority with it; and let this portent of the world be deemed an eclipse of the sun, like others a portent only to the eye.

Phlegon records that, in the time of Tiberius Caesar, at full moon, there was a full eclipse of the sun from the sixth hour to the ninth—manifestly that one of which we speak. But what has an eclipse in common with an earthquake, the rending rocks, and the resurrection of the dead, and so great a perturbation throughout the universe? Surely no such event as this is recorded for a long period."

First things first. Let us orientate ourselves. Africanus lived 160-240 AD. If we place his writings after 221 AD, he is writing about an event equivalent to a modern historian writing about the Napoleonic wars of the early 1800s. I trust that none of us who studied this history in our textbooks at school or university doubted the legitimacy of the account reported by the historians. Let us offer Africanus this clever man who was tri-lingual the same degree of open mindedness.

In his account, Africanus cites another historian, Thallus. Africanus argues that Thallus' account detailing the darkness during the crucifixion had been wrongly attributed to an eclipse. This is significant and strengthens our premise that the *great darkness* at the time of the crucifixion is a factual historical event. Thallus was also a historian, who wrote a three-volume history of the Mediterranean before the Trojan War. The dating of his work is uncertain, but most scholars date Thallus' *History* around the mid-first century, that is, sometime around 50 AD, just twenty years after Jesus' crucifixion in 30 AD. By contrast, some scholars date Mark's Gospel to around 66-70 AD. Hence, it is possible, that Thallus wrote about the darkness surrounding the death of Jesus Christ over a decade before the appearance of the gospels.

Whether post or pre-gospel, either way you have a non-Christian historian writing about a significant event, detailed in three of the gospels, surrounding Jesus Christ. If you were to present a case in court with such consistent and harmonious evidence, the issue being argued would be accepted, and the case will move on. Therefore, if we are to apply the same standards to the *great darkness* issue, we must accept it as proven beyond reasonable doubt, and move on.

What does this mean? What does it prove?

It means and proves that the gospels accurately recorded events as they took place and as such, can be relied on as accurate accounts of what happened.

To summarise; corroboration is key to strengthening the credibility of evidence. The pivotal moment of the Christian faith was the crucifixion of Jesus Christ. This event is documented extensively in the Bible. There is also extra-biblical evidence in connection to one of the circumstances of the crucifixion, notably the darkness that covered the land while Jesus was suffering in agony on the cross. This corroborative evidence concerning the historical moment of the crucifixion is from extremely credible and impartial sources, the Jewish historian, Josephus, who was employed by Rome, and Africanus, a Historian, from the 2nd and 3rd centuries.

Chapter Four

Circumstantial Evidence for the Resurrection

If I took a case to a Crown Court with purely circumstantial evidence, what would you say the most likely outcome would be when the jury issues the verdict to the judge? Would I be able to obtain a conviction? I suspect a lot of people would say, no. However, that is not the case.

If there are enough circumstances pointing to a person's involvement, it is possible to achieve a guilty verdict, even without eyewitnesses or forensic evidence. Such was the case with a murder investigation that I was involved with in 2013. A middle-aged man was found dead in his flat in Walthamstow. He had been renovating his recently purchased home and when found, was still clutching a power tool. Initially the presumption was a tragic DIY accident. However, a post mortem soon revealed a fractured skull.

Due to the findings of the post mortem examination, this investigation was passed on to the Homicide team at Barking as *suspicious* and the case was deemed to be a murder investigation. We soon had a suspect. The next-door neighbour was a drug addict with a criminal record. Certain items were missing from our victim's home such as a TV and laptop computer. We carried out enquiries in some local pawnshops and discovered that our victim's missing property had been sold nearby. We then identified the seller as our suspect who lived next door to the victim. I was one of the arresting officers.

One of the circumstances that played a part ultimately in convincing the jury of our suspect's guilt was that the trainers he wore day in day out were suddenly missing from his flat when we searched it. Most murderers are forensically aware and dispose of clothing and footwear used in the commission of the offence due to the forensic clues they leave.

We had a compelling statement from man who lived nearby. He testified that our suspect wore the trainers every day. Why did they suddenly go missing? Why did the accused offer no explanation when interviewed and asked about the whereabouts of his favoured footwear? He was cautioned in that interview, *"It may harm your defence if you do not mention when questioned something which you later rely on in court."* Still he gave no explanation.

Another aspect that swayed the jury was the fact that despite living next door and sharing a communal entrance, the stench of death in the height of summer, never prompted our suspect to notify the authorities. A decaying corpse in the summer months emits an unmistakable stench that cannot be ignored. Our suspect ignored it. Why?

The entire validity of the Christian faith hinges on the resurrection. If Jesus did not rise from the dead then Christianity is false and is a lie that has duped all believers. However, there is compelling evidence to the contrary.

There is compelling circumstantial evidence that Jesus did rise from the dead

There is compelling circumstantial evidence that Jesus did rise from the dead. Circumstantial evidence is a bit like having lots of pieces of a jigsaw puzzle. When a piece is viewed in isolation, it does not tell you much. When all the pieces are put together and you stand back and view the picture you begin to see clearly what is going on.

I encourage you now to look at the circumstances I am about to disclose and see how they fit together perfectly in pointing towards the resurrection of Jesus being factual. The historicity of Jesus and the fact that he was executed at the hands of Roman soldiers is irrefutable. The first circumstance I will point to is that of the empty tomb.

The Empty Tomb (missing body)

The empty tomb is an important starting point. Just as it can be difficult to prove conclusively a person has been killed without finding a body, it is impossible to prove that Jesus rose from the dead without the empty tomb. So, let us not overlook the important matter of an empty tomb. His followers claimed that he had risen from the dead. Well one fact no one disputed is that the place in which his body was laid to rest was empty.

Despite the tomb being sealed with a heavy stone and guarded by a Roman soldier, inexplicably, the tomb was found bereft of the body. The Jewish establishment paid the guards to spread the lie that the disciples of Jesus came under cover of darkness and stole the body whilst they slept. Something else that should not be overlooked is that the Roman governors were extremely worried about rumours of a messiah, a king of Israel to free the Israelites from Roman subjugation. They would no doubt have searched thoroughly for the body leaving no stone unturned.

Call me a suspicious detective, but if I was interviewing the guard and he claimed that disciples of Jesus stole the body while he slept, I would have a few questions that I would like him to clarify; Like if you were sleeping how do you know it was the disciples who took the body? Where were you sleeping? How much noise does the removal of a stone the size of a door make? Had you taken a powerful prescription medication to facilitate a deep sleep? These starter questions would no doubt multiply according to the answers given to me.

Women as Witnesses

In first century Israel, women did not enjoy the same rights and privileges as men and were the lowest class in society. The testimony of a woman had no weight in law. They were often the property of their husbands. If, as hypothesised by some, the whole resurrection was a scam staged by close associates of Jesus, then which genius amongst the conspirators chose women to be the discoverers of the empty tomb? Surely if the account of the empty tomb had been fabricated the conspirators would have thought up a more believable witness, some male person of apparent good character whose testimony would be taken more seriously than that of a woman.

The inclusion of women as key witnesses is a circumstance that points away from the conspiracy theory. Something else to consider is this. If it was a conspiracy then there would have been a lot of people involved because the conspirators further embellished their resurrection story with tales of post resurrection appearances of the risen Christ.

It is recorded in Paul's first letter to the church in Corinth that Jesus appeared to five hundred people at one time (I Corinthians 15:6). If the resurrection and stories of post resurrection appearances were a hoax, somebody would have broken their silence. Is it not telling that nobody ever did?

The Professionalism of Roman Guards (He was not dead, only appeared dead)

The statement in brackets is an argument called the *swoon theory* often put forward by Muslim apologists. How does this stand up under scrutiny? Roman soldiers were pretty good at what they did. They were efficient at killing. So, when the Roman soldier pierced Jesus with his spear, as he was either dying or already dead on the cross, he would have made sure it was a deathblow.

The penalty for a Roman guard losing a prisoner was a high one; he paid with his life. If the blood loss and dehydration under the Jerusalem midday sun, by some miracle failed to finish Jesus off, then the wrapping of the body in cloth soaked in weighty spices would have surely suffocated Him as the head was completely covered and the movement of the thorax restricted making breathing for a weakened body virtually impossible. There are a billion Muslims in the world who believe the swoon theory because they read it in the Quran. With the greatest respect to the Quran, in terms of textual accuracy, the book is of very little evidential relevance concerning the crucifixion by virtue of the fact it was written some six hundred years after the event.

Saul's Conversion.

The circumstances around Saul of Tarsus converting to Christianity are very compelling indeed. Saul was an archrival and persecutor of the early church and actively pursued Christians, obtaining warrants for their arrest and incarceration. He was a respected Pharisee; well on his way to the very top. Saul was educated by Gamaliel, the greatest Rabbi of his day and leader of the influential Pharisees branch of Judaism. He was trilingual speaking fluent Hebrew, Aramaic and Greek. This is an important point. It shows intelligence and education. Saul was no fool.

Sometime after the disappearance of the body of Jesus, he had a life changing experience whilst on the road leading to Damascus. Saul alleged that Jesus revealed himself to him and explained that by persecuting Christians, Saul was persecuting him personally and opposing the very God he thought he was serving. Perhaps in demonstration of his power, Jesus left Saul blinded by the meeting. Remember Saul was a religious leader and the religious leaders of the time were very big on receiving signs from God. Saul was very hard-hearted and prideful and it possibly took the extreme action by Jesus to get his attention.

Saul's credentials as a persecutor of the early church were very well respected. He was present and gave his approval, when Stephen, the first documented Christian martyr, was stoned to death. However, this apparently supernatural intervention by the resurrected Jesus ended Saul's career as a high-ranking Pharisee. Saul changed his name to Paul and became an apostle to the gentiles (non-Jews). He also ended up writing a large portion of what we refer to in the modern era as the New Testament.

Just to place some context around the transformation, imagine the leader of a terrorist cell plotting with a band of his brothers to attack civilians. Then inexplicably he stops his activities and joins the very people he had been plotting against. Something drastic and supernatural would have had to happen. Such was the case on the road to Damascus with Saul of Tarsus. To be frank, nothing else can explain away Saul's conversion to the very faith he despised and had set out to eradicate.

Lack of Motive

A very compelling circumstance pointing to the truth around the resurrection is the complete lack of motive amongst his disciples to spread the grandest and most outrageous deception in the history of mankind. What did his followers have to gain for staging the resurrection? Becoming a Christian after all was a bad career move.

Straight away, they were insulted as "Christ Followers". They were then banned from the Synagogues which were the cultural hub for all things Jewish. For this reason, first century Christians were accustomed to meeting in homes. Furthermore, most of the disciples did not die naturally; many were executed or were met with horrific ends to their lives. Peter for example was crucified, tradition says upside down at his own request. Paul the apostle, who I have just written about, was beheaded. James was sawn in two. Only John survived into old age and died a natural death. Many Christians sold their property and gave the money to the church so there was no financial incentive. There was no TV, no social media, and no newspapers. Fame and glory was not to be gained out of staging the resurrection.

Telling Details in the Resurrection Account

As a specially trained interviewer with the Metropolitan Police working on Serious Crime, I often interviewed children who had disclosed offences of child abuse. These interviews were always video recorded and would be played in court to the judge and jury. These ABE interviews (Achieving Best Evidence) were the main part of Crown's case. It was very hard to prove a case against a defendant beyond a reasonable doubt when it was the word of the child against the word of the accused.

Something that often helped the case would be a little detail the child would give. It is often a minor detail but one, which would be most unlikely for a child to make up. In John's Gospel, we have one of these minor but ever so telling details that leaves you thinking from an investigators perspective, why would that information be included if the story was made up?

> *Early on the first day of the week, while it was still dark, Mary Magdalene went to the tomb and saw that the stone had been removed from the entrance.* [2] *So she came running to Simon Peter and the other disciple, the one Jesus loved, and said,*
>
> *"They have taken the Lord out of the tomb, and we don't know where they have put him!"* [3]
>
> *So Peter and the other disciple started for the tomb.* [4] *Both were running,*

but the other disciple outran Peter and reached the tomb first. ⁵ He bent over and looked in at the strips of linen lying there but did not go in. ⁶ Then Simon Peter came along behind him and went straight into the tomb. He saw the strips of linen lying there, ⁷ as well as the cloth that had been wrapped around Jesus' head. The cloth was still lying in its place, separate from the linen.

⁸ Finally the other disciple, who had reached the tomb first, also went inside. He saw and believed. ⁹ (They still did not understand from Scripture that Jesus had to rise from the dead.)

¹⁰Then the disciples went back to where they were staying.

There is a lot going on here, but the detail of the folded linen and the placement of them is interesting. If you were making up a hoax story, would you seriously be including detail of folded linen being separated from the cloth?

The Underdog Conquers the Unbeatable

One of my great passions is boxing. However, I never like to see a mismatch where one boxer is totally outclassed and humiliated by the better boxer. The early church of the first century was up against the mighty Roman Empire. This was a complete mismatch. A small band of people, few in number, was up against the strongest and longest reigning empire in history. This was the equivalent of the former undisputed world heavy weight champion, Iron Mike Tyson in his prime going up against a child in nursery.

The Roman Empire pushed Christianity onto the ropes and unloaded everything onto it. The church was defenceless and had to stand and take it. However, try as successive Caesar's might, the church just would not stay down. For each soul that was burned, fed to lions, beheaded, there was another to follow. Eventually, after three centuries of battering Christianity, the Roman Empire ran out of steam and in around 312 AD, Constantine supposedly had a vision of the sign of Christ in a dream, and made Christianity the official religion of Rome.

Just as it would take a nursery child a superhuman effort to beat Iron Mike Tyson,

I submit that it took a supernatural source for Christianity to survive the ferocious onslaught of the mighty Roman Empire, then to come out swinging and win the day by being embraced and made the religion of Rome. Why did Christianity survive when, for many, to embrace it meant persecution and death?

I further submit that no one would die for a lie, or give up their life for a hunch based on a warm feeling. However, a person might have the courage to die for something that they firmly believed to be true based on the evidence of their own eyes and ears. Even after the death of the Apostles, and the people they personally came into contact with, the traditions and accounts and knowledge that they passed down was still strong and common knowledge into the second and third centuries.

The 500 Club

Towards the end of the Apostle Paul's first letter to the church in Corinth (1 Corinthians15:6), he boldly asserts that Jesus appeared to five hundred people at the same time after he came back to life. Paul wrote these words about fifteen years after the events. This is extremely important from and evidential perspective.

500 eye witnesses to the risen Jesus

Firstly, most of the five hundred were still alive at the time of writing and no doubt would have been approached regularly and asked specifically if they had in fact actually seen the resurrected Jesus. Perhaps this begins to explain why the mighty Roman Empire and the influential leaders of Judaism where unable to stamp out Christianity, this off-shoot from Judaism which was threatening the stability of Roman rule in Israel. Judaism was haemorrhaging members from the established religion to Christianity.

What does this mean evidentially in today's *police speak*? Well, if I were to trace and locate every eyewitness, potentially I would have hundreds of MG11s (police term for signed statements with truth declarations). I reiterate, Christianity is an evidence-based faith.

To be candid, there were too many credible eyewitnesses who corroborated what the Apostles were preaching and teaching about Jesus of Nazareth. He was the carpenters son who taught that the Kingdom of God is near, performed great signs confirming his messianic credentials and rose from the dead after being executed.

In summary, I have raised a number of telling circumstances that point to solid grounds for faith in the resurrection. It is an accepted fact that the tomb was empty and the corpse was never found. Christianity maintains that this is because Christ rose from the dead. The conspiracy theory is weak because of the choice of women who discovered the empty tomb, also, it is a fact that not one person ever broke their silence. The *"not dead but appeared dead"* scenario does not stand up under scrutiny. Roman soldiers were no amateurs; they knew how to execute.

I can imagine myself transported back through time and tasked with interviewing the Roman centurion ordered to hasten Jesus' death on the cross. He would be treated as a significant witness and I would arrange for him to attend an interview room where the interview with him would be recorded. When I pose the question to this experienced soldier, hardened by a long tour of duty in Palestine, are you sure Jesus the Nazarene was dead? He pauses momentarily, leans forward and the frown between his eyes betrays his attempt at composure as he recounts his thrust into the side with his pike, the flow of blood and water and through tense lips responds, "Yes, I am damned well sure that he was dead!"

Even if a rare mistake had been made, there is the issue of the suffocation the weakened Jesus would have suffered after his flogging and a day on the cross under the midday Jerusalem sun, due to the weighty spiced linen cloths that covered his head and thorax restricting breathing. Additionally, there are the circumstances around the conversion of the radical Saul, an educated highly intelligent man who positively hated the religion that he was later to embrace and then ultimately lay down his life for.

Then if we add in the complete lack of motive to perpetuate such a grand lie, the little bits of telling detail retold in the resurrection accounts such as the positioning of the discarded burial garments, we begin to have a weighty case of circumstantial evidence pointing to the authenticity of the resurrection accounts.

Finally there is one more circumstance that we need to bear in mind. Why is it, that Rome, the undisputed undefeated heavyweight champion of the world, could not defeat the equivalent of a child in nursery?

Chapter Five

Integrity of The New Testament Manuscripts

If the resurrection of Jesus is the single most important aspect of Christianity, the next subject follows on closely behind. We Christians base our belief system mostly on the twenty-seven books that make up the complete New Testament.

Four gospels, followed by a historical account of how the Apostles began the church and the growth of that church, followed by several pastoral letters, and finally a book of prophesy called Revelation. When I attended court, I would often take with me as part of the case, an exhibit. Typically, the exhibit will be an item found at a scene of a crime that helps to prove the involvement of the accused person. Police will take great pains to ensure that the integrity of the item in question is not compromised and cannot be challenged in court. The history of the exhibit including exactly who has handled it are all carefully documented. That way, when at trial, the judge and jury can trust that the item is the same one seized from the accused or collected from the crime scene.

In the realms of ancient writings, similar questions of integrity are applied. An important question asked is: can we trust the validity of what we now have? Can we trust that the Bible has not been changed? Can we trust that what was written over two thousand years ago has been accurately passed on down the centuries?

An accusation regularly thrown at Christians is that, The Bible has been translated and copied so many times that it is impossible to know with confidence that it accurately records what was first written. Indeed, this sweeping statement has permeated its way into the consciousness of the masses as what we refer to as "common knowledge."

What I investigate in this chapter is how the scholars and experts measure the validity and trustworthiness of ancient writings, and then how the New Testament measures in comparison to the major ancient writings that are universally accepted as authentically preserved. It is comforting to know that there is a system in place involving rigorous tests when examining the authenticity and accuracy of manuscripts.

Firstly, a little background on how we got the New Testament. The printing press was not invented until the 15th century. Prior to that, documents were hand copied. A hand-written copy is called a manuscript. Originally, the manuscripts were written on papyrus, which was a plant-based material and then parchment, made out of animal skins. These were written on and the autographs were meticulously copied. An autograph is an original hand-written manuscript. The custodians of the subsequent manuscripts would not let anyone take on the responsibility of copying these precious writings. The copyists tended to be professional scribes who would copy the manuscripts word for word rather than remember groups of words together.

With the rapid spread of Christianity, the demand for copies of the New Testament writings no doubt precipitated the increase in the number of copies being made to the point where literally hundreds were in existence even as early as the 2nd century.

This is important to remember because of the accusation that the Bible has been changed. A good question in response to this is, when. Was it changed in the 2nd century? If such was the case then this would have had to be a conspiracy involving every custodian of every manuscript that contains the part of the Bible that was changed.

Scholars have been comparing manuscripts for centuries and have found that any divergences are negligible. Differences tend to be errors in spelling or in the sequence of words. For example, 'Jesus Christ' in one manuscript is translated as, 'Christ Jesus' in another. In the history of Biblical study, there has never been a single instance where the core structure and meaning in an authorised version of New Testament manuscript has been altered to mean something entirely different.

If the manuscripts were not altered in the 2nd century, you may well say, perhaps they were changed in the first century. Even less likely a scenario, because in the first century the apostles and their disciples were still around. The eyewitnesses would no doubt have been all over the perpetrators of tampering and adding false accounts into the beloved writings of the apostles. So perhaps they were changed in the 3rd or 4th Century onwards then. This is a sorry assumption in its ineptitude as by the third and fourth century there were far too many manuscripts in existence. Some are still retained today and they all concur. The British Library has many ancient Bibles on display. The top two manuscripts from the 4th century are the *Codex Vaticanus* (325 AD), the cherished property of the Catholic Church, and the *Codex Sinaiticus* (350 AD) owned by the British museum.

The whole "*Bible has been changed*" argument is a gross misrepresentation of the facts. The truth is those who tend to perpetuate this myth simply have not done their research and are demonstrating their lack of reading and critical thinking by merely quoting so called 'common knowledge'. Common knowledge cannot always be relied on as history has proven that sometimes-common knowledge is wrong. For instance, prior to Edwin Hubble's observations in the 1920s, it was common knowledge that the Universe was static. We now know this theory is wrong. Not only is the universe expanding, but the rate of expansion appears to be accelerating.

> The whole "Bible has been changed" argument is a gross misrepresentation of the facts.

Without exception, all the books of the New Testament were in circulation and accepted by the early church in the first century as being of apostolic origin. This adds great credibility to these writings as it demonstrates that far from being embraced by the church because man stipulated that these documents were holy, they were embraced by the church because each could be traced back authentically to one of the apostles. In this sense, it can be proven that they are inspired by the Holy Spirit.

Now that the notion that the New Testament writings have been changed and are unreliable has been exposed as a misrepresentation, let us discuss how the academics and experts measure the integrity (accuracy and reliability) of a manuscript copy. Remember, originals simply did not survive the passage of time due to regular use and the perishable nature of the material. The acid test, if you like, in how scholars and critics alike make a judgement call on how reliable a manuscript is, is to compare the time span between when the events happened to when the details of those events were scribed onto the autograph. (An autograph is simply any original)

For example, the autograph of the gospel of John would be the actual parchment on which the apostle or his designated scribe, wrote down his account. However, if the account of the autograph was first written two hundred years after the actual events, experts would tend to lack confidence in the reliability of the manuscript. This is because the writer would not be writing a witness account. They would effectively be a hearsay witness detailing what they have been told happened, and the details of what they had been told would have been passed down orally. This is where *Chinese whispers* and embellishments can distort the truth.

The second test of reliability is the time between the earliest manuscript copy and the autograph original. The longer the gap between original and copy, the more chance there is of corruption.

Thirdly, critics will consider the amount of attestation in existence from other manuscripts by different writers.

If the manuscript copy being considered ticks all three boxes favourably, then scholars have good reasons to be confident about the reliability and integrity of the document. So, you may well ask how do the twenty-seven books making up the New Testament fare under such scrutiny. The answer is extremely favourably indeed on all three counts.

Firstly, we can be confident that each document was written very close to the events being chronicled. Jesus was executed around 30 AD. History has given us a massive pointer towards the dating of the New Testament writings. We know as a historic fact that Jerusalem was sacked by the invading Roman army in 70 AD. The secular historian Josephus chronicles this event. If the New Testament documents were written after 70 AD, it is astounding that there is not one single mention of this key historical event in any of the documents. What makes this omission even more questionable is that Jesus controversially had predicted the fall of Jerusalem, so the gospel writers would certainly have used this as a further proof that Jesus, the worker of miracles, was also accurate in his prediction about the fate of Jerusalem. (Mark 13) Simply put, it was not mentioned because it had not happened yet. This means that on this one basis alone, we have a compelling reason for an earlier dating for the New

Testament books.

To put some further context around the compelling lack of reference to the fall of Jerusalem in the New Testament, the biblical writers often used key historical events as reference points in their accounts. For example, Luke orientated the foretelling of the birth of John the Baptist, *"In the time of Herod King of Judea"* (Luke 1:5)

The Old Testament writers in particular frequently anchored their accounts around key historical events such as Ezra 1:1: *"In the first year of Cyrus King of Persia...."*, and Daniel 1:1: *"In the first year of the reign of Jehoiakim, king of Judah, Nebuchadnezzar king of Babylon came to Jerusalem and besieged it."*

Indeed, in the latter verse, Daniel set a precedent for us by chronicling a key event concerning Jerusalem at the hands of an invading power. Why would all the New Testament writers omit the latest invasion?

There is also strong internal evidence within the New Testament concerning the early date of their writing. The Book of Acts, for example, records the missionary activities of the early church. This is relevant because it was a follow-up to the Gospel of Luke, written by the same person. The Book of Acts ends with the apostle Paul still alive in Rome. This is indicative of the book being written before the death of Paul, which is generally considered to have been during the Neronian persecution of 64 AD.

The worst-case scenario then, is that all the New Testament originals were written and in circulation within forty years of the events being detailed, certainly within the lifetimes of hundreds of eyewitnesses. I will reiterate, it was not mentioned because it had not happened yet. This means that on this one basis alone, we have a compelling reason for an early dating for the New Testament books. Some have suggested that the earliest New Testament books were written only fifteen to twenty years after the death of Jesus, around 45-50 AD. Certainly, this is the suggested date for the writing of the Gospel of Mark. The fact of the matter is the life of Jesus was written

> **The fact of the matter is, the life of Jesus was written down by eye*witnesses***

down by eyewitnesses (Mathew and John) or individuals who received the first-hand testimony of those eyewitnesses (Mark and Luke).

The writers were all living during the time of the events surrounding Jesus. There is something that should not be missed so I will mention it now. These accounts were written when anti-Jesus campaigners were alive and kicking! They could have contradicted the Gospel's if they were not accurate. The facts speak for themselves; therefore, the silence of the opposition speaks volumes to us who weigh the evidence two millennia later.

Now that we have cleared up the New Testament credentials so far as the early authorship is concerned, for the next test we need to look at the gap between the oldest copies we have and the autographs which are no longer in existence. In the 4th century, a vellum codex became the popular form for copying the New Testament texts. The vellum was far more durable. Our two most valuable New Testament manuscripts in existence today were written on high quality vellum dated from about 325 AD, less than three hundred years after the death of Jesus Christ. This gap to the casual observer may seem a long one. However, for context we need to compare the three hundred years with the time gaps of other ancient writings.

For example, consider the book, Plato's Republic. This work from antiquity has influenced Western philosophers for over two thousand years. No one argues that the book I am reading today has not been accurately preserved and does not accurately represent what Plato wrote in 429 – 347 BC It may surprise you that the time gap between the autograph and oldest surviving copy of Plato's Republic is over one thousand years.

An important point to make here is that there seems to be a gross double standard amongst critics of the New Testament who appear to employ one rule for works from antiquity and then an entirely different standard for the Bible. At the end of this chapter, I have reproduced a table that facilitates comparisons between biblical texts and other well-known and accepted literature. You will see that the Bible compares so favourably in all the key areas where reliability is tested, that it is tantamount to being a complete no contest. In boxing terms, the fight would never be sanctioned by the governing body because the contest is a complete mismatch!

I want to make this point clear because the sad truth is, the average Christian simply does not understand how credible the New Testament writings are when seen against other mainstream accepted literature.

When I finally grasped the reality of this myself, after more than twenty years in the faith, I was completely *wowed*. The last time that happened to me and I *wowed* out loud was at university studying cellular biology and discovering in a lecture how, during the replication of DNA, the cell conducts its own chemical spell check and any DNA strands containing the wrong sequences of genomes, are ripped out. The wonders and complexity of our design for me is the biological equivalent to the encouraging credibility of the New Testament writings. If the average Christian hasn't grasped this important credibility issue, then the chances are your average sceptic hasn't got a clue either!

Now we turn to the test of substantiation from extra-biblical sources. This is where the contest between New Testament literature and other mainstream literature simply gets silly in how one sided it becomes in favour of the Bible. By substantiation, I refer to a double circumstance. Firstly, are there any other copies in existence that say the same thing? Secondly, are there any extra-biblical references corroborating the manuscript being considered? This type of scrutiny is called *textual criticism*, which has the objective of determining as accurately as possible from all the available evidence, the original words of the documents in question.

I will tackle the issue of corresponding copies first. The New Testament writings are the single most copied manuscripts in the history of the world. There are literally thousands of ancient Greek New Testament manuscripts based on autographs written in 45-80 AD. By the 1970s, the actual number of these manuscripts in existence was totalled at 24 633. This number does not include ancient translations into other languages.

In order to contextualise this, consider that for the works of Plato there are seven. Not a misprint, only (7) for this influential philosopher! Another well-known works, the Poetics of Aristotle only has five (5). The nearest rival for New Testament writings in this area is Homer's, The Iliad, which can boast 643 copies. It is not much of a contest is it. The bottom line is this. If the sceptics and critics will not accept the New Testament manuscripts as reliable, they would have to write off all the other ancient writings, which simply do not compare favourably when these *acid tests* of trustworthiness are applied.

Now let us consider the question of extra-biblical references. The Bible is extremely well attested by other writers. The New Testament historically was quoted extensively by writers and church leaders after the completion of Jesus Christ's earthly ministry around 30 AD. So extensive are these quotations that in 1905 a committee was commissioned by Oxford University, to collate them. The committee collected together all the extra-biblical references. They found that nearly all the New Testament books were referred to by these other well-known historical writers from the first and early second century.

The writers I am referring to are Barnabas, Didache, Clement, Polycarp, Ignatius, Ireneas and Papias. If you read or hear reference given to the early church fathers, these are the men being spoken of. A frequent and telling phrase you will find when examining the writings of these apostolic fathers is; *"as it is said in the scriptures."*

The scriptures referred to are, of course, the New Testament writings of the Apostles. This is further compelling evidence for the early writing of the documents collated into what we now call the New Testament.

In summary, we can be very confident in the integrity of the New Testament. The manuscripts have been copied more extensively than any other work from ancient times and great care has been taken to transpose them accurately. In all areas of textual scrutiny, the New Testament outshines manuscripts from other genres. So far as the early dating of the New Testament books, the evidence that they were written in the first century, during the same generation as the eyewitnesses, is overwhelming. This gives the New Testament outstanding credibility. So far as textual integrity is concerned, the New Testament documents are as good as it gets.

Sir Frederick Kenyon *(15 January 1863 – 23 August 1952)*, the former director and head librarian of the British Museum, was generally recognised as one of the foremost experts on ancient manuscripts in the world. Shortly before his death he wrote this about the New Testament documents.

> *"The interval between the dates of the original composition and the earliest extant evidence becomes so small as to be in fact*

negligible, and the last foundation for any doubt that the scriptures have come down to us substantially as they were written has now been removed. Both the authenticity and the general integrity of the books of the New Testament may be regarded as finally established"
(The Bible and Archaeology, pp288-89).

New Testament writings compared with other accepted manuscripts

Author	Date Written	Earliest Copy	Approx Time Span between original & copy in years	Number of Copies	Accuracy of Copies
Lucretius	died 55 or 53 BC		1100	2	–
Pliny	AD 61-113	AD 850	750	7	–
Plato	427-347 BC	AD 900	1200	7	–
Demosthenes	4th cent. BC	AD 1100	800	8	–
Herodotus	480-425 BC	AD 900	1300	8	–
Suetonius	AD 75-160	AD 950	800	8	–
Thucydides	460-400 BC	AD 900	1300	8	–
Euripides	480-406 BC	AD 1100	1300	9	–
Aristophanes	450-385 BC	AD 900	1200	10	–
Caesar	100-44 BC	AD 900	1000	10	–
Livy	59 BC-AD 17	–	???	20	–
Tacitus	circa AD 100	AD 1100	1000	20	–
Aristotle	384-322 BC	AD 1100	1400	49	–
Sophocles	496-406 BC	AD 1000	1400	193	–
Homer (Iliad)	900 BC	400 BC	500	643	95%
New Testament	1st cent. AD (AD 50-100)	2nd cent. AD (c. AD 130 f.)	less than 100 years	5600	99.5%

*Information from the CARM Christian Apologetics and research ministry
http://carm.org/manuscript-evidence

There are three key points below to draw the reader's attention to in the above comparison chart;

1. The time gap between the autograph and the earliest copy for the New Testament manuscripts is on average one millennium closer.

2. The number of copies of New Testament manuscripts in existence far outweighs the fifteen well-known and accepted manuscripts in the comparison.

3. The chart lists only the Greek New Testament manuscripts. If you include the copies translated into other languages then, you reach somewhere in the region of 24 000 copies made. *(This is where the argument that the Bible has been changed falls down under scrutiny.) The 24 000 copies are consistent with only odd variants which are minimal and do not alter text meanings.

If the argument that the Bible has been corrupted is to be accepted, we have to ask when and how. All 24 000 copies would have had to be changed. That is a lot of people conspiring together!

Chapter Six

The Evidence of Design

Psalm 19

> *"The heavens declare the glory of God;*
> *the skies proclaim the work of his hands.*
> *Day after day they pour forth speech;*
> *night after night they reveal knowledge.*
> *They have no speech, they use no words;*
> *no sound is heard from them.*
> *Yet their voice goes out into all the earth,*
> *their words to the ends of the world."*

Something I find intriguing about this psalm is the way the writer encapsulates how the heavens are themselves a testimony to a creator. This psalm was written over three thousand years ago. Yet even before astronomy developed as a natural science and before the invention of the telescope, the writer had figured out the sheer magnitude of the sky at night. I have heard it said that there are more stars in the universe than grains of sand on our planet. That makes for an infinitesimal number, which I simply find incredulous, especially when you consider the vast distances between the stars, which is measured in terms of light years, in comparison to the way sand is compacted together.

The psalm writer, as he looked up into the heavens from the plains of the Holy Land, free of the light pollution that blights modernity, was *wowed* at the expanse of the stars and their number.

When we look up into the night sky, we are looking at heavenly bodies ranging from between four to millions of light years away. A light year is the distance light can travel in one calendar year. For some perspective, consider that light travels at 186,000 miles per second. So if a star one hundred light years away exploded into a super nova fifty years ago, we would not know about it for another half a century. Effectively when we look up at the sky at night, we are looking back in time. Surely, the sheer magnitude of the universe is in itself an indicator of the existence of a creator, and the power of that creator. The number of stars and galaxies and the vast distances between them are a little clue as to how unfathomable God is to our mortal minds.

From a very young age, I recall an interest in the heavenly bodies. I had a friend named Andrew who lived on the estate where I grew up. He was a year or two older than me and owned a telescope. One freezing cold winter night, we were on my 2nd floor balcony kitted out in hats and scarves, we took turns to view the rings of Saturn and at least two of the moons of Jupiter. So began my interest in science. I was in absolute awe. It is said in some quarters that science and the belief in God is incompatible. I refute this notion absolutely. Science tells us how, The Bible tells us who and why. For instance, we know from science that the atmosphere of the earth was once thick and dense as it was forming. We know from the Bible that God said, *"Let there be light and there was light"*, clearing away the gases, allowing the light from the sun and moon to reach the surface of the earth. In his book, <u>The Genesis Enigma</u>, Dr Andrew Parker does a great job detailing how the book of Genesis inexplicably gets the sequence of events right in the evolution of the planet earth and the life on earth. He asserts that this is remarkable because the writer of Genesis had no right to get it right, since the sciences of geology, biology and astronomy were three thousand years in the future.

In this chapter, I discuss the evidence of design from the world around us starting by introducing the *Intelligent Design* theory, as a scientific argument. Just look at some of the clues from within the realms of the natural sciences, such as the complexity of a cell and some of the components inside the cell such as the Flagella. I also look at some of the laws of nature and how these laws are proof of intelligent design.

Let me start by using the analogy of my car as an example of evidence for design. Suppose I were to pick up a sceptical companion and convey them to a place of their choice. Our destination is a good hour away and we strike up a conversation about creation. During the conversation, I try to convince my friend that evolution makes no sense and the evidence of design is everywhere. My companion disagrees with me and says no chance!

Evolution is scientific and is proven, survival of the fittest and random mutations and all that. I then say to my companion, perhaps you are right, this car evolved, I found it parked up in a forest and I firmly believe that over millions of years this car formed randomly. My sceptic friend would no doubt consider that I was being sarcastic and dismiss what I had just said. The car was clearly designed and then made by an intelligent agent. We can even name the organisation the makers and designers belong to, Nissan. Quite rightly, my sensible sceptical companion does not entertain my foolish and somewhat facetious comment.

Now consider this, one single cell inside a typical human tissue, is far more complex in design than my Nissan motor car. Before the invention of powerful atomic microscopes, is was widely believed that the cell was a very simplistic structure consisting of a cell wall containing cytoplasmic fluid, and a nucleus at the heart of the cell. We now know that the cell is a complex structure that is not unlike a warehouse consisting of a great deal of organisation and complexity with different sections and molecular machinery. The cell even has a currency. Without that currency absolutely nothing happens. That currency is called Adenosine Triphosphate (ATP) which is the fuel driving all the cellular processes such as chemical synthesis, building molecules required for muscle contraction, nerve impulse propagation. ATP is found in all life forms. How can it be that we readily accept a car will not randomly form, and yet we cannot accept a human body needs a designer. The alternative to the human body having no designer is that it randomly formed and pieced itself together. This when you think about it is as absurd a notion as my car evolving in the forest by itself.

Let us now have a look at the evidence for design, as a scientific theory. A criticism of Creation as a theory about the beginning of the universe is that it is unscientific, immeasurable. However, a new strand of scientific theory has gained momentum, that of Intelligent Design Theory (I.D). Intelligent Design Theory is the idea that life, the universe, and certain aspects of nature, can best be explained as having an intelligent cause. It stands in contrast to theories about naturalistic causes that suppose all designs are random involving undirected processes.

For a theory to be accepted as scientific the theorist needs to demonstrate that in arriving at their position, four elements are present.

1. An Observation
2. A Hypothesis
3. A Testing of the hypothesis
4. A Conclusion based on the test results.

Observation

I.D theorists observe the types of information produced by intelligent agents such as a computer programme or a language. These are clearly systems, which adhere to rules. As part of their study, the I.D theorists will place under close scrutiny many parts of a specified design that has a specific purpose or role to play. The theorists will observe how the intelligent designer will re-use parts over and over again in different types of designs. For example, the wheel will find itself on a motor vehicle, a trolley, a bicycle, a travel case, and airplane, a wheelbarrow, a hospital bed etc. The design will be re-used in various items designed for different purposes.

Hypothesis

An observable object in nature if designed, should display the same characteristics as objects we know were formed at the hands of intelligent agents. A designed object would be expected to display a high degree of organisation and complexity whilst adhering to set patterns that are unlikely to have come about by chance. They also predict that objects in nature would display the same indicators of an intelligent designer's work: Natural objects would be arranged with parts that have specific purposes. Parts would be re-used over and over in other objects in nature.

Testing

An Intelligent Design theorist can test their hypotheses by using a very simple method. Using the hypotheses that designed objects display evidence of certain kinds of information, I.D theorists can study objects in nature to check for evidence of this information existing in them. When the I.D theorists study things in nature, they observe high levels of organisation and complexity that are unlikely to have come about through chance and conform to set patterns. They observe in nature, evidence of the work of an intelligent agent: Natural objects have a specific arrangement with parts for specific purposes.

In biological objects, I.D theorists observe many machine-like systems. They have specific arrangement of different parts that are all necessary for the function of the biological object. In fact, further experimentation has shown that if even one of the parts of many biological objects were changed or missing, the biological system would no longer work. These are called "irreducibly complex systems."

Conclusion

Many objects in nature were designed by an intelligent agent. Objects in nature display the same kind of information that objects known to have been designed by an intelligent agent do. There is no other process known that can explain how this information came about in nature. Therefore, an intelligent agent must have designed them.

The theory of evolution teaches that new organisms do not suddenly arise but come about gradually due to random mutations that prove beneficial to the organism. These mutations, it is said, are caused by natural selection. This is what Charles Darwin said about his own theory:

> "If it could be demonstrated that any complex organ existed which could not possibly have been formed by numerous, successive, slight modifications, my theory would absolutely break down" (<u>On the Origin of Species</u>, Cambridge, MA: Harvard University Press, 1964, pg. 189).

Evolution is just a theory, and there is an enormous chasm between what evolutionists claim can be achieved through random mutation and natural selection and what these elements of the biological process, can actually achieve.

The scientist Michael Behe is credited with introducing the theory of Irreducible Complexity. Behe argues that some biological systems simply could not have evolved because they display such complexity that if a single component were missing they simple would be unable to function.

Furthermore, the more complex the organism, i.e., contains numerous irreducibly complex parts, the less the chances of all of them arising together.

To emphasis his point, Behe uses the example of a spring loaded mousetrap. It only has five parts to it. A platform, spring, holding bar, hammer and catch. If one of these parts were missing, it cannot function as a mousetrap. The gravity of this theory should not be overlooked. If this scientific theory is correct, then according to Charles Darwin's own words, the theory of evolution is null and void.

The presence of irreducibly complex systems points to the presence of a designer of those systems since they are too complex to have randomly mutated into their present form. The human cell contains some very complex molecular machinery. Behe looks at several examples from nature of irreducibly complex systems. Among them is a particular bacterial component, the flagellum. These are tiny hair-like filaments used by some bacteria to swim in whatever environment they are found. In 1973, it was discovered that some bacteria literally use the flagellum as a propeller, rotating them around an axis rather than simply wriggling them as was previously believed. These flagella have been measured at a speed of 100,000 rpm.

> *The presence of irreducibly complex systems points to the presence of a designer of those systems*

They achieve this by using a cellular filament connected to a drive shaft-like device attached to the cell wall. The machine like complexity does not end there. There is a motor rotating this observable drive shaft. Each part of this propulsion system is unique and the flagellum simply could not function as a propulsion system if one of the components were absent. Like the propeller on a speedboat requires some fuel in a tank, the drive shaft of the flagellum is fuelled by acids, and certain proteins appear to control the system. Scientists have identified around fifty different proteins that are involved in the operation of this very tiny propulsion system. Genetic knockout experiments show that all of these unique parts are necessary for the system's function as a rotational propulsion system.

I digress away from the microscopic to the astronomic. It is now widely accepted that the universe, far from being something that has simply always existed, had a definite beginning. This beginning it is said was a huge cosmic explosion, the "Big Bang". Indeed, there are clear traces that this occurred. The simplest one is the observation that our universe is an a state of expansion and that objects moving away are gaining momentum, indicative of an explosive beginning.

If it is to be accepted that our universe had a definite beginning then it is reasonable to think that something caused this beginning. Creationists maintain that this cause was an intelligent one.

There is also much evidence of design to be obtained from our observations of our universe. So much so that, it has been proposed that the universe displays signs it has been specifically designed to support life here on earth, the Anthropic principle. Some people, when they consider the size of the universe really struggle to believe that all this was created specifically for little insignificant us. After all our planet is a mere pinhead in an ocean, and we as living souls are much smaller than that.

However, I discovered a very interesting point recently. In the grand scale of things when comparing the size of elements from the tiny electrons and quark particles that make up atoms, through to the star giants of our universe, the human body is exactly half way up the chart *pro rata* in terms of size. I personally found this really surprising and it placed our position in the universe in a far greater context. Relatively speaking, we are not as insignificant in terms of size as many of us believe.

The position of our own galaxy in the universe is also an indicator of planning. Some parts of our universe are very hostile with galaxies in close proximity to each other tearing themselves apart as their gravitational forces clash and interfere with the order within each independent system. Imagine the devastating consequences if our own earth's orbit around the sun was interfered with by the gravitational pull of another star, forcing the earth from its natural course away into a diverse movement. It is known that in our own solar system there is a very narrow corridor in which life on earth can survive. It is not a coincidence that the planet Earth is alone in our own solar system in sustaining life. A small shift closer to the sun, we would all fry, a small shift away from the sun we would all freeze, the end of life on earth either way.

This positioning of the earth and its location in proximity to the Sun is also indicative of design. Isaac Newton is generally accepted to be the genius that figured out the laws of gravity. Newton argued that the stability of the planetary system was dependent not only on the universal laws of gravity, but also upon the precise initial positioning of the planets in relation to the Sun. He explained this as follows;

> "Though these bodies may, indeed persevere in their orbits by the mere laws of gravity, yet they could by no means have at first derived the regular position of the orbits themselves from those laws... [thus] this most beautiful system of the sun, planets, comets, could only proceed from the counsel and dominion of an intelligent and powerful being."

The location of our own sun, is also indicative of careful planning. Astronomers have detected around a hundred planets in the universe that orbit around stars. Our own star, the Sun, is unique in that it is stable and caught in a regular position, which is maintained.

It is positioned in exactly the perfect spot in our own galaxy known as the Milky Way, to avoid destructive gravitational pulls and harmful radiation emissions from star giants. This is a similar scenario to being located in the eye of a storm.

The waters are calm whereas the surrounding waters are raging high, reaping terrible chaos. Were our sun to be in another spot within the galaxy our solar system would be in absolute chaos, rendering the formation of a life-sustaining planet impossible.

Speaking of sustaining life, the earth happens to possess an abundance of the commodity best suited in the whole universe for life to develop and survive. Water is vital to life. Its properties seem to be exactly right for maintaining life. It is the best solvent (something that dissolves other things) that we know of. It is also uniquely suited to protect developing life forms and provide their habitation. It provides a stable temperature and protects from harsh elements.

In his paper on I.D Theory, Behe, details the unique qualities of water:

That solid water, unlike most elements, floats in liquid water is important to life as well. If it did not float, there would be no ice caps on the earth's poles. The ice would sink to the bottom of the ocean. As soon as it sank, the water at the surface would freeze and sink. Eventually the sea would freeze solid and everything in it as well. The same would happen to rivers and lakes. Instead, water freezes and floats, insulating the water below and preventing it from freezing and allowing life in that water to survive. The cause of this phenomenon is the unique way water crystallises as it freezes. All other naturally occurring substances are denser in their solid than their liquid form. Only water is less dense in its solid form than its liquid.

Water's high boiling point is important to life. It means that water condenses at a much lower temperature than other substances. For example, hydrogen sulphide, which is heavier than water, boils at 88 F. If the boiling point of water was different one way or the other, there would be no liquid water on earth and thus no life, as we know it.

In conclusion, whether we look at the minute atom, which itself mimics a planet surrounded by moons, or the wonderful complexity of the human body, from the cell through to the complex biological systems making up the human body, or the enormity of the stars and galaxies of our universe, the arguments for an intelligent designer cannot be ignored. When discussing the evidence of design, it is hard to do such a major topic justice in just a single chapter, but I hope to have awoken you to the idea that nature and the natural sciences give testimony to an intelligent agent being at the root of the building blocks for life.

PART TWO

My Journey To Faith

Chapter Seven

A Need for Answers

"The words of the Teacher, son of David, king in Jerusalem:

"Meaningless! Meaningless!"
Says the Teacher.
"Utterly meaningless!
Everything is meaningless."

What do people gain from all their labours
at which they toil under the sun?

In the Old Testament, there are some books of wisdom, Proverbs being the most popular. After the book of Proverbs is a *section* called Ecclesiastes. Above is how the book of Ecclesiastes starts. This is a very appropriate text to begin my journey. It sums up very well my thinking and what fuelled my own need for answers to the questions, is there a God, and why am I here?

The futility of life! The Hebrew word used, translated as 'meaningless' in the above passage, is *hebel*, the literal meaning is vapour or breath. Have you ever sat and pondered if there is more to life? If life is in reality, a mere breath, or a vapour that appears and goes in an instant, what is the point? Is that even fair? What was God playing at and why am I here?

Certainly, I was asking myself these very questions. Some great athletes who achieve their dream of reaching the very top of their chosen sport have spoken about the initial elation of victory, being almost immediately dampened with sense of anti-climax. They contemplate, "So is that it? What next?" I recall Linford Christie sharing this in a TV interview shortly after winning the men's 100m sprint title at the Barcelona Olympics in 1992.

In 2008, I experienced similar emotions immediately after completing an epic cycle ride. Along with a team of five cyclists and three support helpers, on a cold windy dreary afternoon, exhausted after two weeks of cycling over hilly terrain, we arrived at John O'Groats; the top of Scotland having departed from Land's End the South Western most point at the bottom of England, fourteen days earlier. The epic cycle journey took us the length of Great Britain covering over one thousand miles; one thousand and twelve was recorded on my personal odometer. This was the fulfilment of a dream and was the culmination of the better part of a year of planning and training.

Something that had started as cycling the twelve-mile commute from my home in Hackney to my place of work in Tooting Broadway, evolved into the epic length of the United Kingdom Challenge. I remember my initial elation at having accomplished the task was quickly replaced with a sense of anti-climax. The mission was finished and the adventure over, and I would soon be back doing the day job. I was now part of an elite few, less than 1% of the population of the UK have ever accomplished this task, and I was now numbered amongst them, part of a unique group, so it took me by surprise when I started feeling deflated.

I begin my story before I came to a belief in the existence of God, whilst on honeymoon with my wife, Jean. We were married on 9th September 1989. We had a church wedding although at the time of our marriage neither of us was particularly religious, only attending church for weddings and christenings. We were both open to the existence of God, but had neither the faith conviction nor belief to devote our lives. We also had no understanding of what a devoted life in the modern era looked like. Life was good and we had every reason to be happy. This is an important point to note, as there is a perception that people turn to religion only out of a desperate need when life takes a turn for the worse.

Perhaps bereavement, relationship breakdown, major health problem and so on, religion is seen as a crutch for the weak. Such was not the case for me. I was a young healthy man, gainfully employed as a Field Sales Executive. The proud possessor of a brand-new company car, delivered with about twenty miles on the clock. I even had my own business cards. Wow, I thought I had arrived! Not bad I thought, for a poor boy from Hackney.

I grew up in relative poverty when compared to my peers at school. I say relative, because now I am accustomed to how children in the third world live. I was positively rich. However, compared to other children in the UK things were hard for me. I did not have many clothes and at one time, I possessed only one pair of shoes. They were a pair of brown shoes procured from a jumble sale. Knowing that my mum was struggling to make ends meet I did not trouble her with the predicament of my treasured brown shoes, when they became worn out, so I pressed on wearing them through thick and thin.

The eyes of my own children have glazed over when I recounted the tale of only owning one pair of shoes that had a hole on the sole. I was fine in dry weather but when it rained, the foot in the holed sole got very wet. Squelchy squelch as I walked along in the rain. I look forward to passing on this very tale to my grandchildren who are frequent beneficiaries of a new pair of shoes from grandma and grandpa.

At the beginning of my story, I was gainfully employed and married to my childhood sweetheart and recently we had moved into our own a council flat, and the icing on the cake, we already had two wonderful healthy sons. We enjoyed a good life. However, there was uneasiness within me. In the back of my mind was the notion that no matter what we achieved in life, at the end of the day, the dreaded fate of death was inevitable. I did the maths around lifespan versus time span of the universe and I found the minute fraction human life was reduced to, in comparison, somewhat depressing. If I were fortunate, I would live for three scores and ten years then be on borrowed time.

Some contest that the universe is billions of years old. Seventy divided by billions is a very small fraction. In the grand scale of things, we are only here for a few microseconds and then we are gone. Like an early morning mist, the *Hebel* of Ecclesiastes.

I recall feeling if that was it; a short life followed by eternal death meaning we were born to live and then die and be gone forever, life was a cruel joke! What was the point of living in the first place? I have a vivid memory of my wife and me as newlyweds sitting outside a Tearoom in Paris and having this conversation. Our lovely relaxing time together was interrupted with a sudden gloomy silence as we momentarily contemplated this futility of life. We quickly snapped out of it and continued to bask in the ambience of our honeymoon, but the dissatisfaction concerning the futility of a life destined to amount to nothing more than dust remained deeply embedded in my mind.

I think the yearning for meaning and knowledge of why we are here, has been with me since childhood. I recall having conversations with my mother about the existence of a god. My mother was not a religious person. Mum's grandfather, Fred Porter, who raised her, had taken her to church as a child. Once when aged about five, he had shown her a picture of Dante's, *Inferno* and told her that, *"bad people burn in hell."* This *fire and brimstone* approach to God had the effect of turning my mother off religion from a very early age.

I recollect as a teenager probably around the age of eighteen, becoming interested in the idea that we as living beings are actually spirits, i.e., living souls. Our bodies are just vehicles to move around in.

I read a book on Astral Projection. Simply put, this is the belief that the spirit is separate from the body and this separation can be practiced, to produce an *out of body* experience. On one occasion, I remember lying on my bed in darkness and consciously trying to remove myself from my body. Something quite remarkable happened that I cannot explain. I had a tremendous sense of being lifted outside of my body into space. I was surrounded by the darkness of space and recall feeling anxious as I was separated from my physical body.

There was a clear corridor of light, a striking illumination against the backdrop of dark space. This passageway linked me through space back into my body. However, I had ventured so far into space that I could not actually see my physical body. It occurred to me that I may not be able to find my way back and I panicked. I felt in the realms of the supernatural and this sensation was alien to me. In that moment, an instant, like the snapping of my fingers, I was back in my body, flesh and living soul reunited.

> **I was surrounded by the darkness of space and recall feeling anxious as I was separated from my physical body.**

I have never ventured to try that again and strongly suspect that most people who try astral projection will not experience anything like the *out of body* experience I managed to achieve, in this sense, I think that I am an exception to the rule. Perhaps that experience served the purpose of heightening my sense that there was more to life than flesh and blood; a spiritual place outside the realms we know.

I do also recall that my mother was a keen astrologist for many years when I was growing up, and well into my adult years. She had also tried out contacting the spirit world. She once had a frightening experience that she spoke about to me. She never went down that Road again and I steered well clear. Perhaps this knowledge is what precipitated my panic when I had my own *out of body* experience.

Searching

"Ask and it will be given to you; seek and you will find; knock and the door will be opened to you. ⁸For everyone who asks receives; the one who seeks finds; and to the one who knocks, the door will be opened." (Matthew 7:7)

This is my *go-to* verse in the Bible when I am sharing my faith with others. What comforts me about this passage is that it is loaded with a promise. If you seek God, you will find him.

I remember as a young man, asking God to prove to me he existed. To show Himself to me, manifest Himself in a vision; then I would believe. Nothing happened. No supernatural experience and certainly no vision from God. However, now I am acquainted with the Bible, I am relieved about this. When God's prophets received visions, they were often left trembling in fear. Daniel for instance on receiving a revelation from God concerning future world powers was left ill for several days.

Saul who met Jesus on the road to Damascus was blinded. The shepherds in the fields were terrified when an angel appeared from nowhere to announce the birth of

Jesus. Another problem with sitting back and waiting for God to reveal Himself is that it overlooks the fact that God has already revealed Himself to mankind and we now have a whole library of revelation, the sixty-six books that make up the complete Bible. Furthermore, sitting back and waiting is a bit half-hearted. God offers some advice for those who are seeking in the Old Testament through the prophet Jeremiah.

> "You will *seek me and find me when you seek me with all your heart.*"
> Jeremiah 29:13.

The feeling of futility consigned to the back of my mind on honeymoon, stayed with me and was what triggered my interest in religion and my quest for answers. Sometime after returning to England from our honeymoon, my quest for answers gained momentum and I became involved with the Jehovah Witnesses.

Previously I had avoided them at all costs, as I simply did not have the time to chat for ages on the doorstep. I would not dream of inviting them into my home, as I would never get rid of them. However, I was now thirsting for answers.

On one occasion, I was standing at the sink washing dishes when I saw a group of them walking along my road going from door to door. I remember hoping they would knock on my door too, as I had much I wanted to discuss.

I had several Bible studies with an old man called Stanley Palmer. I also attended a few meetings at one of their meeting venues known as a Kingdom Hall. I recall that after the meetings during my discussion with members I would be asked the question, "How long have you been in the truth?" I think I blended in well and some thought I was already a part of the movement.

Lots of what I studied made sense to me and on the surface; the movement looked very slick and polished. I recognised that they were extremely serious about sharing the gospel with their door-to-door knocking. Many of them deliberately took on part-time jobs. They were called *Pioneers*. They worked reduced hours so they could devote time to working for God in their Street Ministry of door-to-door evangelism and the associated Bible studies that this generated. This was commendable and I respected them for it.

I showed so much zeal for knowledge that another Jehovah Witness I came to know through work, procured for me a two-volume encyclopaedia (Insight from the Scriptures). These were not meant for non-members, so I was somewhat in a privileged position to have been permitted to purchase these volumes.

I never became a Jehovah's Witness. A few things bothered me about the religion. At the helm of the Jehovahs Witness movement, is the Watch Tower Society, which effectively dictated doctrine and beliefs. I recall spending very little time reading the Bible as opposed to a great deal of time reading their leaflets and books. Also, something really bothered me. What Gospel would I be preaching if I became a Jehovahs Witness?

The Bible they use is called the New World's Translation of the Holy Scriptures. They are not permitted to call it a Bible because it is not an authorised version. Quite simply it has been changed by the Watch Tower Society to harmonise with their theology system and core doctrine.

I refer to Galatians Chapter one. This letter was written by the Apostle Paul. In it, Paul warned about alternative gospels.

This is what Galatians, says about this in chapter one;

> *^{6}I am astonished that you are so quickly deserting the one who called you to live in the grace of Christ and are turning to a different gospel— ^{7}which is really no gospel at all. Evidently some people are throwing you into confusion and are trying to pervert the gospel of Christ. ^{8}But even if we or an angel from heaven should preach a gospel other than the one we preached to you, let them be under God's curse! ^{9}As we have already said, so now I say again: If anybody is preaching to you a gospel other than what you accepted, let them be under God's curse!*

This put the fear of God in me. If I preached a false gospel, I would become a false prophet and be under a curse. Paul was so adamant about this that he said it twice. I just could not get my head around the alternative gospel issue and this was ultimately the big sticking point for me. The more I picked at and unravelled the teachings of the Jehovahs Witnesses, the more problems I found in their theology. Essentially what I found with the Jehovah Witnesses was that they were sincere but, from what I could make out, just plain wrong.

The Bible demonstrates that when true prophets of God predicted things they happened. The Jehovahs Witnesses have on their track record at least five predictions about the second coming of Christ that failed to happen. They have made lots of assumptions about what the Bible means and turned those assumptions into doctrine. For example, a very basic one was that John the Baptist was beheaded on King Herod's birthday, therefore though shall not celebrate birthdays. The Bible does not teach this but they insist on it. Also, in their thinking, they are in the truth, and therefore, everyone outside of their movement is part of Satan's system of false religion. For this reason, the average Jehovahs Witness will not listen to you. After all, why should they? They are already in "the Truth" and you, according to their theology, are a part of Satan's system.

As I recall, to become a baptised Jehovah Witness takes months, and involves a tremendous amount of studying. The Bible demonstrates that conversion was often very quick. A Christian later pointed out to me that the longest conversion referenced in the Bible took three days.

Rightly or wrongly, I still have a bit of a soft spot for Jehovah's Witnesses. They were the first group that I came across as a started searching. During my time of studying with them, I grew greatly in the knowledge of God. Nevertheless, here is a health warning. When I later came across a true disciple of Jesus, using a proper authorised Bible, and sound doctrine, my own theology took a lot of unpicking before I could make the step of being baptised into Christ.

Sometime after deciding that the Jehovah Witness route was not for me, I changed jobs. I was doing reasonably well as a Sales Executive but my earning potential was limited. I responded to a newspaper advert and applied for a position with a Life Assurance company. I was successful in my application so I gave up my guaranteed salary and took on what was a commission only job, against the advice of Jean who is always very cautious about big decisions.

Over the years, I learned the hard way to listen to my wife. I learned from experience that it can, and usually does go horribly wrong when I ignore Jean's advice. She is very perceptive and intuitive. We have a private joke between us. Often when we are having a discussion and Jean is giving her input I will stop and in a soft voice mouth the words *"listen to thy wife,"* as if a third party, a guardian angel, was speaking to me.

Unfortunately, on this occasion, I did not listen. I was lured into this precarious situation by the promise of high earnings, and the dream of providing financial security for my growing family. One slight problem though. I had very few personal contacts and I went into the Financial Services Industry off the back of the first economic recession of my lifetime. My personal contacts were not professionals, they were mainly young and still finding their feet. Financially this was the worst decision I ever made and it caused great stress and anxiety as I struggled to pay bills.

As a self-employed Financial Consultant with no basic salary, reliant on commission only, I had to generate my own business by cold calling. I found this really hard to do. Our income reduced and our debts increased. The venture was doomed to fail. I ended up getting part-time work as a debt collector, then a Loans Agent to supplement my unpredictable income. In fact, it was as the Loans Agent that I met the Jehovah Witness who procured the Insight from the Scriptures volumes for me. It was whilst I was working as a Financial Consultant that I met someone who was to have a significant impact on my life and greatly accelerated my conversion process. His name was Ranald MacDonald.

> I believe that God sends us certain signposts in life

I believe that God sends us certain signposts in life and to this day I still find it amusing that God sent 'Ranald, which is an anagram of Randal. I joke with Ranald that he has my name spelt wrong!

I was seeking God and I was on the same Induction Course as Ranald, a disciple and *fisher of men*. During the icebreaker session, we all had to say something about ourselves. Ranald listened intently to what everyone shared as each person spoke. After I spoke about myself to the group, Ranald decided that I was the open person, the one to reach out to. During the coffee break, I asked Ranald what he was up to at the weekend. This was his opportunity and he shared that he was a

> *I was seeking God and I was on the same Induction Course at Legal & General as Ranald, a disciple and fisher of men.*

Christian and would be attending Church.

Bearing in mind, I was seeking God, I think my eyes must have lit up and I questioned Ranald more about his church and beliefs. I recall being greatly impressed by the evident enthusiasm he had for his faith, which I found rare and very refreshing.

One early seed was planted in me whilst I was still working as a Financial Consultant. I recollect an incident that occurred whilst I was standing on the platform at Tottenham Court Road station. A casually dressed bearded man suddenly started to preach there and then to the waiting commuters. He stood out because he was surrounded by smartly dressed, suit wearing city workers. He basically delivered a quick sermon. The message was about heroes. He asked the question who the heroes are in the world today? He said I want to talk to you about my hero, a man who lived 2000 years ago. He went on to preach about Jesus.

I was deeply impressed by his boldness. I recall he was heckled a couple of times. I also recall that he held a dignified composure until the heckling was finished, and then continued with his preaching. This man's preaching demonstrated to me that there were some very committed Christians around. One of the reasons I almost became a Jehovah's Witness was the fact that they were so committed and I was under the impression there was no other committed group in a world that had turned its back on God.

I was clearly wrong and this stranger's preaching reassured me that the Jehovahs Witness movement did not hold the monopoly on commitment. A quarter of a century later, I wonder what the man is doing now. I wonder how many times he has preached publicly. I also wonder how many seeds were planted by him on that crowded platform that day. Could it be that I was the one person in the crowd inspired by his preaching? Could it have been for my benefit he was inspired by God to preach on that day to help me break my ties from the Jehovah Witness cult?

Just as I would be deeply encouraged, a few years later at Alexandra Palace by the young man who reminded me that I once shared my faith with him on route to him becoming a Christian, I would love to encourage the Tottenham Court Road Station preacher about how impacted I was that day by his bold spirit-filled public preaching.

Chapter Eight

When Trouble's in My Way

"We all have a story brothers and sisters. Are you sharing your story? Have you told your family members, your children? Do they know what you were like before? Get open get real."

There is a song we often sing at our church services the title of which I have chosen for this chapter. The song is about a spiritual God-reliant response to the troubles of life. However, it has not always been the case for most Christians that we responded to trouble in a peaceful manner or to the everyday troubles of life in a spiritual manner. The above words were preached by an elder and evangelist from the South East London, Church of Christ, Mr Toks Sowoolu, at Logan Hall in central London on Sunday 19th February 2019, two days prior to my 53rd birthday. It struck me that the middle-aged man sitting listening intently was a world apart from the man I once was.

Toks was preaching about the transformation of character from worldly self to Christian self in a Christ-centred life. His point was that our genuine transformations are in themselves a testimony to the power of the Word of God to change people for the better. Toks is a naturally gifted preacher who speaks with great power. I pay special attention to him when he speaks.

It is the transformation I see in men and women born again into the new life that genuine Christianity offers that gives testimony to the power of the Word of God to change people for good. Notice I said, *genuine Christianity*; this is not to be confused with the brand out there that merely requires the odd attendance at church, the odd prayer and good deed, but no transformation of character.

I refer to this brand as "Churchianity". It is to be avoided at all costs and must never be confused with the real thing, which has real power to change lives. *Churchianity, has no power in it, and is a lukewarm brand of so-called Christian practice* abhorred by Jesus.

> **Churchianity, has no power in it, and is a lukewarm brand of so called Christian practice**

> *"For the word of God is living and active, sharper than a double-edged sword. It penetrates even to the dividing of soul and spirit, joints and marrow, it judges the thoughts and attitudes of the heart. Nothing in all creation is hidden from God's sight. Everything is laid bare and uncovered before the eyes of him to whom we must give account."* (Hebrews 4:12)

God's word is not dead! It is alive and can precipitate great change in people. It triggered such a change in me that I offer my own transformation in character as part of my grounds for my faith in the Bible. Before becoming a Christian, I had to make some adjustments. I had some things of which I needed to repent.

There was certainly a struggle between the *good* in me and the *bad* side to me as I grew through my teen years and into my early twenties. I became a father at the age of nineteen, unmarried.

I realise now that some great good came out of this even though the situation was far from ideal. Having a child dependent upon me had the effect of taming my wild side. After one brawl in the street with a group that had robbed my best friend, Kelvin, of our takings after a fund-raising event, one of them shouted to me as he ran from us; "We know where you live we know who your family are."

This really got my attention, and made me question my willingness to involve myself in trouble. During this period, there was most certainly an internal battle going on. Who was I? Was I just a hard man reaping my own retribution when people took liberties and were disrespectful to me or a responsible upwardly mobile career man building a family?

The biblical word for repentance is from the Koine Greek language the New Testament was originally written in. The word is *metanoia*. Greece, under Alexander the Great, had conquered much of the world and built a huge empire, that is why koine Greek became the common language of the Greek empire, and remained the common language when Rome became the new world super power, and ultimately the language the New Testament was written in. The word, *metanoia,* literally means to change direction. God requires a *metanoia* in the person who follows him. *Metanoia* is a change of thinking and a change of life. A mind-change! It is the measure of the validity of a person's repentance. No change in life style, then I would question if the individual has repented. Biblical repentance should be followed by a very noticeable change in behaviour and values.

One of the areas in my life that needed to change was my propensity towards violence if provoked. "If" and "provoked" were the operative words as I was not one to go looking for trouble. Indeed, I have always been a conflict avoider.

> One of the areas in my life that needed to change was my propensity towards violence if provoked

Usually the confrontations occurred on the football field. I was a combative defender and my game was based on speed and robust tackles. My aggressive style of play periodically provoked confrontation. But there were occasionally other incidents too, outside the realms of football. When involved in a confrontation, if push turned to shove, I was not averse to start throwing punches.

One incident happened when I was on my way to work. I was an Administration Trainee at the time, employed by IBM, working on the Southbank. I was suited and on my way to work one morning. The platform was very crowded and commuters were herded close together and in each other's space.

A man dressed in combat fatigues and bigger than me decided to get hands-on and shove me to one side as we were going in opposite directions. This was a 'liberty' and I was not having any of it. I remonstrated with him. Of all the days this person chose to bully me, he chose the morning after the Marvin Hagler versus Tommy Hearns, world middleweight title fight.

Marvin Hagler, was a ring legend, world middleweight champion. Tommy 'the

Hitman' Hearns was pound-for-pound the most feared puncher in the world and had taken out old *Hands of Stone* himself, Roberto Duran, another Hall of Fame legend in his previous fight.

Hearns was a knockout specialist, also a world champion. He had stepped up in weight to challenge Hagler in a super fight; champion v champion. The fight only lasted three rounds, but it was three of the most exciting rounds ever. Both men went at it toe-to-toe from the opening bell and both had a *no retreat, no surrender* approach. There was no science just attack! attack! attack! As they landed bombs, each man wobbled. Hagler sustained a bad cut and the referee took several looks at the injury and was close to stopping the fight when Hagler floored Hearns. The Hitman had been out gunned.

I listened to this fight live on the radio and I think it finished at about 5am UK time. By the time I was making my commute to work, I think the adrenalin rush from the fight was still in my blood.

Now back to the incident on the underground. My adversary was unapologetic and squared up to me. I think he thought I would back down from the bigger man. He was wrong! As push turned to shove, I started to throw punches. Initially I was punching thin air but as I marched forward, he backed off and backed off until he was backed up against the wall of the underground station and unable to retreat any further. It was at this point my punches started to land on him. I recall we then stopped fighting.

> As push turned to shove, I started to throw punches.

It dawned on me that I was up against a bigger guy dressed in a combat jacket whilst dressed in my only suit for work! I came to my senses. At that age, late teens early twenties, I was still trying to raise my game. I was conscious that I was a poor mixed-race boy from a single-parent family in Hackney trying to better myself in what was essentially a white middle-class working environment. Working as a trainee Administrator for IBM, I already felt out of my depth at work and this was not doing my self-esteem any good. At school, I had fights to even scores, but this was not school anymore. I was trying to be respectable and lose the *street* inclinations in me.

It must have dawned on my adversary that I was serious and he had taken on more than he had bargained for. As I looked at him, I recall saying, "are we done?" We parted company going our separate ways. The flurry of punches lasted only a few seconds, not long enough for a significant crowd to form and no real harm done other than slight bruising and both of us looking a bit dishevelled. I recall being somewhat surprised when I arrived at work to notice a slight bruise under my eye. I had not felt a punch.

Around this period, I had purchased some music playing equipment, which I had saved up for. My younger brother, Martin, four years my junior, was sufficiently impressed by our new powerful sound system that he invited over one of his local peers, a lad named Raj to come to our home and listen to it play. I recall that Raj looked at the equipment in such a way as to make me uncomfortable. A few days later, I arrived home and our house had been burgled, no more music equipment.

I was so upset and deflated. I remember speaking to a neighbour who was pretty switched on with a finger on the pulse on what was going on with the local youngsters. Raj's name came up. I recalled the covetous look as he peered towards my equipment and put two and two together.

I rang Kelvin, explained the situation and we plotted our next move. After making some enquiries and finding out where Raj lived, we showed up on his doorstep. Raj, an Asian, was amongst the first crop of Asian youngsters who spoke with the accent of the younger urban black kids. His mother, however, who opened the door, was a tiny woman who spoke with a strong Asian accent.

I asked Raj no questions and simply told him "I want my stuff back, I know you are involved get it for me now."

He looked terrified and his mother looked up at me pleaded with us "please don't hurt him." Raj came with us to a flat around the corner. He exited the car and disappeared into a block of flats on Upper Clapton Road. About five minutes later, he

> He looked terrified and his mother looked up at me and pleaded with us, "please don't hurt him."

re-appeared carrying my treasured graphic equaliser and amplifier. We got the equipment loaded into the car and then took him for a drive. He was not off the hook yet. After all, he had taken a *liberty* and needed to be taught a lesson.

We ended up in Wanstead or somewhere by a forest area. I punched him a couple of times, more for effect than out of anger and then with Kelvin's help picked him up and threw him in the lake. We did this, as it would have been highly embarrassing to have driven all that way and just let him off the hook. After walking back to Kelvin's car, we sat down. It was misty and freezing cold. Raj had crawled out of the lake, soaking wet, placed his hands in his pockets, and started to jog his way home. He looked a pitiful sight. Kelvin and I looked at each other, looked at Raj and were on the same page. We pulled up beside him told him to get in. We gave him a lift home. I think the pleadings of his mother were still whirling around in my head. So much for being East End tough guys, we had soft centres!

I think my credentials as a hard nut had been cruelly exposed. Yes, I could see the red mist and launch into someone in anger, but plotting to harm someone and then carrying out that plan just wasn't in me. What this incident taught me was that I did not really have the stomach to hurt someone. I was too empathetic.

I discovered later from Martin that another friend of mine, Noel, had turned up at our home after Kelvin and I had departed. Unknown to me, Martin had given him the heads up that we were plotting something and there might be trouble. In hindsight I am glad that we left before Noel arrived as I have a hunch Raj would not have benefitted from a lift home that night. Noel and I were close friends growing up, but we were to end up on two very divergent paths.

It was not always the case that my altercations were born out of anger or to even scores. I recall a night I intervened to protect someone. I was making my way home from work on a D6 bus from Limehouse through to Hackney. At the time, I was running a Loans circuit for a licensed credit broker. I was a Collections Agent. I started this venture whilst working for Legal & General as a Financial Consultant, as it supplemented my commission only salary.

Usually, I would use my car but on this evening, my vehicle was out of action. Fortunately, my area was so condensed, I could walk the circuit and collect payments. I was at the back of the bus on route home on completion of my night's collecting, and

I observed a group of teenagers get on board; there were about four or five of them. This was before the days of Oyster cards, and one of their number must have tried to pay a child's fare. The English bus driver politely asked the individual his age, to which he received a torrent of abuse in what I can best describe as a combination of youth culture lingo and Jamaican Patwa.

The driver then said quite reasonably, words to the effect of, "Excuse me, are you swearing at me? I'm not swearing at you or being rude to you so please don't be swearing at me." The group then went onto the upper deck without further incident, or so I thought!

After just one stop, the likely lads reappeared and stood by the door at the front of the bus. However, when the doors were opened they remained rooted to the spot and waited for other passengers to alight. I knew instinctively, what was about to unfold. The group suddenly set upon the driver reigning down punches and spitting at him. Fortunately, there was a partial screen between the driver and the group so he had some protection. I was so enraged; the driver for no reason other than doing his job was being viciously assaulted.

I could not contain myself. I must have bridged the gap from rear to the front of the bus in a split second. Shouting like a crazed man, "Nooooo!", I launched kicks and punches into thin air in the general direction of the group of assailants. I half expected to be confronted with a knife and the fear of this ensured a bloodstream full of adrenalin.

To my surprise within seconds, they had all cleared off the bus. In my mind, they were getting off to regroup and come back for me. Not wanting to be cornered on a bus, I jumped off to continue the intervention or run like the wind if a knife was involved. I looked left and right, forward and back, there was no sign of them. I was completely perplexed at how quickly they had disappeared into the night, like rats down a hole in the ground.

Clearly, when confronted with an unknown quantity, they were not quite so brave. I got back onto the bus and asked the driver if he was ok. He angrily stated, "No I am not ok!"

He was clearly shaken by the incident and was still livid at the sheer injustice of it. After a few moments he regained his composure and then said, "I am so glad there was someone like you on the bus."

> "I am so glad there was someone like you on the bus."

By the time I got home, I was still shaking. I think I was as angry as the driver was at the sheer senseless and needless violence. I was also still in fight and flight mode. Perhaps it was this incident that first planted the thought in my mind that I could become a police officer and serve to protect vulnerable people.

The Dream

One of my favourite films is The Matrix starring Keanu Reeves. The film details a man's search for the truth,. As he searches he realises that everything he had believed to be true was really a lie. People were not actually living out their daily activities they were effectively in an induced coma plugged to a machine energising the world of their captors; evil machines had taken over the world, bent on destroying all human life. Eventually, his search brings him to a character named Morpheus who is the leader of the resistance with the goal of setting people free from their induced comas.

There is a scene in the film where Morpheus offers Neo a choice, the blue pill that will send him back to blissful ignorance, or the red pill that will show him the truth. The red pill came with a health warning, you may not like what you find and there is absolutely no going back. Neo chose the way of truth with all the baggage the truth pill carried. The *red pill - blue pill* scenario is analogous of the tussle I had as a young man over which route I would take in life.

I am not usually one for dreaming. However, for several years from my mid-twenties onwards, for possibly a decade or more, I had a recurring dream. The dream was a bad one, a real nightmare.

In my dream, I was with Noel and we had killed someone. We had concealed the body by wrapping it inside a carpet inside a terraced house. In the dream, it was always during the night when we were at the house. Each time I woke up I would be carrying this big dark secret. My heart was heavy and I was in fear of discovery and my life being ruined. I also felt ashamed that I had allowed myself to get embroiled in such a sordid event.

> Each time I woke up I would be carrying this big dark secret. My heart was heavy and I was in fear of discovery

The routine was always the same. As I broke out of my slumber and realised I had been dreaming, the anxiety and heavy heart morphed into sheer relief that turned to joy as I came to the realisation that it was all just a bad dream. However, the dream was so vivid that on occasions, I would wonder if I had actually been involved in this and due to guilt and trauma, erased it from my mind as a protective mechanism.

Several years ago, I was at home in the kitchen, probably taking care of the important ministry of cleaning the dishes, and the news was on TV. From the living room, Jean blurted out in surprise "Randal, come here!"

Noel (who had turned up at my house when Kelvin and I went looking for Raj), was on the news. He had been found guilty at crown court of being involved in a killing. It was a sordid tale of what was believed to be a gang-related feud, due to a drug deal gone wrong. I later found out from the internet that it was believed by the Crown Prosecution, the victim had not supplied the correct quantity of drugs he was supposed to and the gang lured him to a meeting and reacted with violence. It was thought that the victim had a health condition and the beating that ensued possibly caused his heart to fail.

The body of the supplier was discovered in a barrel in the countryside. The exact cause of death could not be determined and intent to kill could not be proven hence Noel's conviction was reduced to *manslaughter* and he was sentenced to only six years. Noel accepted the punishment and did not disclose who else was involved. No other suspects were identified and arrested.

Growing up, Noel was a very close friend. We were in and out of each other's homes and did a lot together until Jean and I started our family. We lost contact after he moved to West London and then I uprooted to Essex. I do now wonder if the recurring dream was somehow linked to the internal battle that was going on inside me over the route I was going to take in life. Certainly, Noel and I journeyed on the same road together for a few years, before we separated onto different roads.

There are countless examples in the Bible of God speaking to man through dreams. It has occurred to me that perhaps my recurring nightmare served the purpose of God showing me the sort of life I could have led, had I not chosen to become a Christian. For sure, the majority of non-religious people are not bad. However, for me, with such a strong instinctive inclination towards anger and vengeful thinking when wronged, I think only the fear of God could change me.

> I think only the fear of God could change me.

This idea that God was showing what could have been was further enhanced when I joined a Homicide Investigation team in 2011. When I first arrived, I was at a bit of a loose end for a while without much responsibility. I joined a group of officers who visited schools and gave presentations to teenagers concerning the law around Joint Enterprise. This is a controversial legal doctrine, which dictates that if two or more people are present when a person is stabbed for example, then all those present can be arrested and potentially convicted of the murder under joint enterprise. The controversy around this law is that prisons up and down the country are filled with young men who were present at an incident where someone was killed and they ended up being charged with murder, even though they maintained their innocence.

In some cases, those convicted professed they were not even aware that the person they were with, who inflicted the fatal wound, had a weapon. I became part of the concerted efforts by the Metropolitan Police Service to educate youngsters around the perils and pitfalls of gang involvement and carrying weapons. The reason this is so profound for me was that my friend, Kelvin, who was best man at my wedding, was arrested on suspicion of murder the late 1980s.

The incident was a carbon copy of the scenario that I was warning about. He was at a party in Wood Green and one of the partygoers had been robbed of a gold chain. The victim came into the party and gathered some friends. Kelvin who was at the party tagged along to see what was happening. Tragically, things rapidly escalated, the young man who committed the robbery was stabbed, and his injury proved fatal.

I recall finding out about the incident when going to work at the Community Centre where I had been hired as Security after the teenagers had started to run amok and staff were feeling intimidated. One of the Community workers, Jackie, who was very close to Kelvin, informed me that the police had attended Kelvin's home looking for him and had searched his room and seized clothing. She asked me if I knew anything. I reassured her that I knew nothing and I was pretty sure that if Kelvin had any involvement in something so serious, I would know about it, as we were very close. I could tell from Jackie's face that she knew something I did not.

Jackie then filled me in that before Kelvin had flown off on a planned holiday to Portugal, he had confided to her that he was present during the stabbing. Upon Kelvin's return to England, he was arrested at the airport on suspicion of involvement in the murder and remanded in custody where he remained for several months until the trial. I visited him in Brixton prison whilst he was on remand. Ultimately, Kelvin was found not guilty and acquitted. The point is the bond between us was tight; we grew up together from nursery school to secondary school.

I have absolutely no doubt that had I been in Wood Green that night with Kelvin, I too could have been drawn into tagging along with the crowd, even if only to keep my mate out of trouble. When I addressed all those children in schools and colleges, perhaps I was successful in turning some away from the gang and weapons trap. If my influence was effective for just one youngster, the time was not wasted as far as I am concerned.

By the time I reached my thirties, the *metanoia* in my character was a complete turnaround. Fortunately, what happened on the football field remained on the football field. What happened with the burglar of my home in Hackney remained in Hackney without police involvement. Growing up in Hackney, you just did not talk to the police. They were the enemy. I had been stopped and searched on a few occasions, sometimes when I was with Kelvin. So, we understood the culture of why young black men in Hackney were extremely wary of police. I recall when there were riots in Tottenham, and a police officer named Keith Blakelock, was brutally murdered by a mob on the Broadwater Farm, a notoriously rough council estate.

The very next morning I was walking near Chatsworth Road in Hackney, on route to the Chatsworth Community Centre where I was working as a security guard. Two young police officers came around the corner. They were speaking but as our paths crossed, they fell silent. The tension between us was tangible. I so wanted to speak to them and say how sorry I was about what had happened to their colleague. But as we passed, I said nothing. They remained silent and refrained from making eye contact, paused the conversation they were having and turned the corner. I was frozen by the fear that I would not be taken seriously. I was a young black man and I felt sure they would associate me with the young black men who were involved in the Broadwater Farm riots, and not welcome my attention.

My wife and I took our granddaughter, Laila, to lunch in Muswell Hill for her tenth birthday a couple of years ago. On route back to the car, I spotted a memorial stone for PC Keith Blakelock on the Broadway, which was the area he served as a *beat officer*. I stopped for a moment and paused to read the writing on the stone. What happened to him that night still saddens me.

A few years ago, I had to attend the Broadwater Farm Estate whilst conducting enquiries in relation to an investigation. As I walked through the estate and saw the pantheon of stairways my mind drifted back to what it must have been like on that fateful hate-filled night, and as I walked past a green area, I wondered if that was the spot where my fellow officer was felled and killed.

By 2002, I was fortunate to have an untainted record and had never been arrested. At the rather mature age of thirty-eight, having been a Christian for a decade and certainly over a decade since I had last had a violent exchange, I joined the police; a changed man.

I was once held as teenager for criminal damage and theft. I came out of the cinema with Noel and another friend. Hyped up by the film, possibly a martial arts movie, I had the bright idea of punching my fist through the wooden board of the cinema's shop, and grabbing a fistful of chocolate. Technically this was a burglary. Two employees at the cinema were nearby and grabbed me. I was taken to the office where I was held until the police arrived. When they did, after a conversation with the employees that had caught me, the police decided to let me go without arrest on the basis that the Rio Cinema Manager did not want to press charges. That single moment of stupidity could have cost me my future career as a police officer.

I did not take the decision to join the police on a whim. I thought about it long and hard. I asked several friends of their opinions about whether I should apply. Without exception, the responses I received were positive. Almost as soon as the question had left my mouth, I was being told to "go for it, it is you." The positive feedback instilled confidence that I was making the right decision so I applied and after a long drawn out process, was successful.

A few years ago, whilst I was working at Hertford House in Barking on the Homicide investigation team I joined, I had a consistent training regime, spent a lot of the time in the gym pumping weights, and gloved up doing bag work. I let off a lot of steam punching that bag, occasionally when upset about some interactions with colleagues that I felt had taken a liberty with me. I think my placid approach and reluctance to get involved in confrontations was often interpreted as weakness. Consequently, sometimes I felt that liberties were taken in tone and attitude when speaking to me. The punch bag got the full brunt of my frustration. One of my colleagues who shared gym time with me remarked that if ever I "lost the plot it could go a bit wrong for someone."

I admit that this comment pandered to my ego and I thought to myself, "I resemble that remark." I still have it in me. But through the power of God's word and the Holy Spirit, the wolf is caged. Indeed, I have never retaliated in anger as a Christian. However, I admit I have come close on occasion. I am a driver and have lost count of how often some disgruntled man has threatened to punch my lights out over some minor infringement.

Standing up to an aggressor is not necessarily a challenge for me it is instinctive. Far more of a test for me is having a courageous conversation with someone close with whom I am in conflict, or a Christian brother with whom I need to raise an issue, maybe behaviour that is out of place for a church member, a poor example, or dare I say it, sinful and wrong.

Back in 2016, I was working as a local taxi driver in Basildon. This was during the period of my career break when Jean was seriously ill. I was reversing my vehicle along the taxi pickup point where ASDA shoppers wait for pick up, to collect my fare who was waiting with her shopping bags. I recall a man in a mini bus wanting to edge his way into the slot I was reversing into. However, undeterred I continued to reverseand exited my vehicle and opened the boot in readiness to load the shopping. The driver of the mini bus was clearly annoyed that I had stopped him from illegally parking so that I could do my job. He made some rude gestures whilst mouthing his frustration. I looked at him and pointed to one of several clearly marked signs, which said *TAXI'S ONLY*.

He responded with what we call, "road rage" and edged the front of his vehicle progressively and *intimidatingly* closer to me, sandwiching myself between the back of my car and the front of his. Not one for being easily intimidated I placed both hands on the front of his mini bus and shouted "TAXI's ONLY!" This prompted a sudden halt as he hit his breaks. There was an audience of a dozen people all waiting to be picked up, and I had made a bit of a spectacle by raising my voice.

The errant driver jumped out of his vehicle and rushed aggressively towards me. Fearing I would be assaulted and with adrenalin flowing through my veins, instinctively, in fight and flight mode, I gave him a flurry of pre-emptive punches to his solar plexus and his head, dropping him instantly to the ground drawing a huge gasp from the crowd of onlookers.

> I gave him a flurry of pre-emptive punches to his solar plexus and then to his head dropping him instantly to the ground

Are you shocked at this disclosure? Actually, I am going to stop there. I have been deliberately mischievous. Although I have recounted a true event, it never ended the way I have just described it. Everything after placing my hands on the front of the mini bus and shouting, "taxi's only", never actually happened outside of the confines of my mind. What actually happened was the driver got his shopping loaded, mouthed some unsavoury words and gestures to me before driving off. I turned the other cheek and carried on with the business of loading my passenger's shopping into the boot of my car. I then drove off making polite conversation with my passenger.

Nevertheless, what I described after that point is how I replayed the event in my mind. I use it as a pretty typical example of how, although outwardly I have usually acted appropriately and shown restraint, inwardly I have often burned with anger and allowed someone else's errant actions to spoil my day. When Jesus admonished his followers to forgive their enemies, he did so for a reason.

I do confess that my Christian life has been plagued with bad thoughts as I have carried interactions with me and replayed them in my mind. Often making up my own version of events in my head of how some incidents ended with me reaping my own terrible vengeance on some ungodly Pagan who dared to disrespect me. Even though physically I have refrained from retaliation, mentally I have often resorted to violence as I have taken revenge into my own hands, and fallen back mentally into not accepting disrespect and striking out in anger.

In later years as I have grown more in tune with the Holy Spirit, I have realised that these thoughts are damaging to me. Each bad vengeful thought is like swallowing poison. I have really struggled to change this. I have learned to hate this sinful part of my character. When we hate something, we get rid of it. That is what I strive to do. The "honour Jesus" comment I employed to stop the *red mist* when I played football has now developed into a mantra that I repeat when faced with aggression and the selfish thoughtless attitudes of others. "It is to the Glory of God when I honour Jesus and overlook an offence." This helps me refrain and stay at peace within myself.

For many years as a Christian, I felt that there was a lack of evidence of the Holy Spirit working in my life. In recent years, as I have striven to eradicate the sin of vengeful thinking from my heart, I have a much stronger sense that God is working in my life. To put it another way, *Randal Porter,* with his sinful nature has stepped out of the way and God has started working in his life.

> **For many years as a Christian, I felt that there was a lack of evidence of the Holy Spirit working in my life**

When I think about it, bearing in mind where I grew up and my early negative experiences with police officers and the trouble I could have fallen into with the number of times I had altercations, I find it quite remarkable that I became not only a police officer but a successful one progressing to a substantive detective working on Specialist Crime. I have sometimes felt like a fish out of water. I have sometimes questioned if I made a mistake becoming a police officer, especially when my health has suffered due to the sheer stress of the job, manifesting in crippling migraines and anxiety. One thing I have always been confident about however, God is in control and is pulling at the strings.

Chapter Nine

Metanoia

So far as the misdemeanours on the football pitch were concerned, I was not exactly out of control. Over a period of fifteen years in football, I was only sent off on a handful of occasions. I did play a bit on the edge though with lots of robust tackles to win the ball for my team, and I was occasionally susceptible to seeing the *red mist*.

If I am honest, I suppose I relished being the "hard man" of the teams I played in. At the time around my conversion in 1992, I was twenty-six years old and playing for a team called *Sentinel*, in the Dagenham & Essex League. I had resumed playing after a break of about six years during which I had concentrated on bodybuilding and martial arts.

I trained in Tae Kwon Do and then a variation more akin to kickboxing, Choi Kwon Do. I became very competent and enjoyed the explosive kicks and punches and the self-confidence that came with my training. I even developed my own technique, which I called the "lightning strike." I would practice this move repetitively against a manikin and in thin air against imaginary opponents.

It was a simple move where I would stand passively with my weight shifted onto the back foot. My left hand over my right wrist, left foot forward in a very relaxed and passive stance, shoulders hunched. As I am approached and threatened by some imaginary foe, I would then shift my weight onto my front foot whilst rotating my right hip forward. I would then deliver the lightning strike into the solar plexus, (soft tissue area of the sternum central to the rib cage) or, as the punch was delivered from below hip level, it would be an explosive uppercut.

What makes the move so dangerous is that it is unexpected. No forming the praying mantis position, announcing an intention to strike, as demonstrated in the popular film, Karate Kid! Just an out-of-the-blue concussive blow, keeping the element of surprise. There have been a couple of occasions over the years when I have stood toe to toe with an aggressor and in my mind asked that question "shall I?"

Fortunately, I have always refrained, shoved my ego back into the cage and held my peace; at least as far as my actions were concerned though often inwardly seething with anger.

One of my reasons for being confident about joining the police was my martial arts training, and track record of being able to handle the physical aspect of the job if things got rough. However, once I started my police training, and became aware of the laws around the use of reasonable force and proportionality, I soon realised that all my martial arts techniques were completely useless. The police have approved methods for the use of force and restraint, which do not involve flurries of punches and kicks!

I missed the football so much I resumed playing. The martial arts had a very positive impact on my game. No longer a cumbersome centre-half, I now added balance and poise and started playing in more attacking positions.

My new team had a couple of young forwards aged seventeen or so whom I nick named the *young guns*. They were very skilful and caused a lot of problems with their pace. I took it rather personally as the team's enforcer when the opposition took liberties and tried to kick them out of our games. I recall one occasion when we were playing a friendly game. The other team had the biggest man I had ever seen on a football field. Possibly six foot six and thighs like tree trunks. He had no skill and just wandered around the pitch kicking our players. I nicknamed him *Attila the Hun*.

I recall one of his teammates kicking out at me after I had cleared the ball away. It was so blatant. He had completely ignored the ball, which was an irrelevance and simply tried to kick me. This was a liberty I simply could not tolerate so after jumping back to avoid being kicked I landed a right hook flush on his jaw as he was turning away. Within seconds total mayhem!

This was a liberty I simply could not tolerate, so after jumping back to avoid being kicked, I recall landing a right hook flush on his jaw.

His father was standing on the touchline and in the brawl, that ensued had his hands around my throat. The opposition team descended around me and my own teammates came to my defence. The lad I had punched had to be taken to hospital with a suspected broken jaw. I had not meant to hurt him, it was an instinctive *red mist* reaction.

After being pulled away from the drama whilst standing waiting for things to calm down, Attila, having realised his teammate had been hurt, started striding purposely towards me. There were two brothers in our team both rugged defenders. Keith, the older and bigger of the two saw Attila striding towards me and gestured to his brother. My teammates stood shoulder to shoulder with me, one on each side. No words were exchanged and the three of us just stood in silence eyeballing Attila. He got the message and walked off in another direction. Even a man of his intimidating size did not relish the prospect of taking on the three of us. I can tell you that I was one so-called "hard-man" who was extremely grateful for the company of my teammates at that moment in time.

The match was abandoned due to the trouble that ensued and I received a six-week ban for violent conduct. I served my suspension and resumed playing. The cost to me was that I missed the League Cup Final as it fell during my ban period. However, as I progressed in studying the Bible I bear in mind that I made a great effort to curtail my short fuse. I realised that it was somewhat hypocritical to be praising God at a church on one day and then lashing out in anger on another.

My cunning plan to keep calm and curtail my temper was to wear a wristband during games. On the wristband I wrote in bright colours, *honour Jesus*. I remember I used a turquoise felt pen to inscribe the words on my band of honour. The idea being, each time I felt the red mist rising, I would glance at the wristband as a reminder. There was one game when this worked a treat.

We were involved in a bad-tempered League match and one of the opposition players kicked one of our "young guns" in the air for the umpteenth time. The referee blew his whistle for the penalty. The offending player then kicked the ball away onto the next pitch as our player tried to retrieve it to place onto the penalty spot. This was a double liberty and I paced purposely towards him to remonstrate.

He saw me coming towards him and I think players on both teams braced themselves for what was going to kick off between us. As we confronted each other, I clenched the fist of my right hand looked down at the writing on the wristband and informed the player, "Jesus loves you man". If I had punched him, I do not think I could have had as great an effect. He stopped instantly then slowly turned and walked away looking somewhat perplexed.

> "Jesus loves you man!"

After the game, I was one of the last to enter the shared dressing room as I was assisting with the responsibility of removing the nets from the goal posts. He was talking about what happened and was reciting all the things that had been said on the football pitch to him over the years. None of which I would venture to repeat. "Jesus loves you man" was a new one to him. I was not yet a Christian but this was possibly the first occasion in my life that I evangelised and spread the good news! We were playing Sunday League football and one of his teammates quipped hey Randal, shouldn't you be at church on Sundays?

There were other skirmishes over the years as I refused to accept liberty taking. I do not want this to degenerate into a pantheon of my misdemeanours so I will draw a line here. But you will no doubt get the essence from what I have shared that I could be quite volatile when provoked and needed to make some adjustments in my life before I became a Christian.

I became increasingly attached to the church that Ranald had introduced me to. It was called the *London Church of Christ* and met at the Odeon on Leicester Square.

I recall the first time I attended. It felt strange leaving my wife at home. At that time, Jean had no interest. She had seen me go through the Jehovah Witness phase and move on. I think she felt that it would be the same with this new group of religious people. It felt even stranger attending a church service that was being held in a cinema.

I recall that I was on the central line train making my way to church and contemplating returning home. I doubted that I had the capacity to become a Christian and thought that "Bible bashers" were weird. Did I really want to become one. Just at this very moment, a young woman named Siobhan spoke to me. She explained that she was on her way to Leicester Square for a church meeting and enquired as to whether I would be interested in coming along with her. I explained that I was already on my way there. I think her intervention stopped me from getting off the train and we travelled the rest of the journey together. On arrival, Siobhan introduced me to a brother and disappeared into the auditorium to take her seat.

I remember being so impressed at the singing and how the men and woman sang different harmonies, complementing each other. I was also impressed by how everyone seemed to know all the words to every song. My previous experiences of church songs had tended to be the Vicar and the *old lady behind me* being heard, and everyone else mumbling along half-heartedly. This experience was very different. Each worshipper was belting out the songs at the top of their voices. Another very pleasant surprise was the preaching, which would make me laugh and then search my heart in the next instance.

There is an amusing anecdote to my repentance story. The question asked of me in the changing room after the "Jesus loves you man" incident proved prophetic. I was issued a very simple challenge in one of my Bible studies before baptism: so, on Sunday, what is it going to be, church or football?

Clearly, I could not be in two places at once so I quit playing football on Sunday and said my goodbyes to my teammates. I assume word had got around the league that Sentinel's robust 'Number 5' had left the team to pursue church. The next time my teammates lined up against one of our rivals, Wall End Wanderers, a tough team from Manor Park in the East End, one of their number approached Jason, my former teammate, and enquired, "Is it true that Randal has found God?"

"Is it true that Randal has found God?"

Baptism

> [26] Now an angel of the Lord said to Philip, 'Go south to the road – the desert road – that goes down from Jerusalem to Gaza.' [27] So he started out, and on his way he met an Ethiopian eunuch, an important official in charge of all the treasury of the Kandace (which means 'queen of the Ethiopians'). This man had gone to Jerusalem to worship, [28] and on his way home was sitting in his chariot reading the Book of Isaiah the prophet. [29] The Spirit told Philip, 'Go to that chariot and stay near it.'
>
> [30] Then Philip ran up to the chariot and heard the man reading Isaiah the prophet. 'Do you understand what you are reading?' Philip asked.

> [31] 'How can I,' he said, 'unless someone explains it to me?' So he invited Philip to come up and sit with him.
>
> [32] This is the passage of Scripture the eunuch was reading:
>
> 'He was led like a sheep to the slaughter,
> and as a lamb before its shearer is silent,
> so he did not open his mouth.
>
> [33] In his humiliation he was deprived of justice.
> Who can speak of his descendants?
> For his life was taken from the earth.'
>
> [34] The eunuch asked Philip, 'Tell me, please, who is the prophet talking about, himself or someone else?' [35] Then Philip began with that very passage of Scripture and told him the good news about Jesus.
>
> [36] As they travelled along the road, they came to some water and the eunuch said, 'Look, here is water. What can stand in the way of my being baptised?' [38] And he gave orders to stop the chariot. Then both Philip and the eunuch went down into the water and Philip baptised him. [39] When they came up out of the water, the Spirit of the Lord suddenly took Philip away, and the eunuch did not see him again, but went on his way rejoicing.
> (Acts 8 26-39)

On reflection, I realise now that during the period of my baptism, the London Church of Christ was having what we refer to as a *campaign month*. That is focused and organised evangelism with lots of invitation church services and Bible studies.

One of the meetings I attended was what we refer to as a *chariot ride*. The message was based on the book of Acts Chapter 8, the Ethiopian eunuch who responded to the Gospel by being baptised immediately. A man named Michael O'Hanlon studied the Bible with me on a regular basis. Jean would not have been very interested or receptive to inviting a stranger into our home for Bible study. This would not have gone down very well with her so we arranged to meet in the home of Mary, a member of the church who lived near me.

Michael was working for the church at the time as an 'intern'. He loaned me a book. The title was not very subtle. It was something like, *Why I Am Not a Jehovah Witness*. The book exposed the false doctrines perpetuated by the Jehovah

Witnesses. The book detailed at length the deity of Jesus Christ.

One night I was reading the book. I remember it vividly. I read into the early hours of the morning, everyone else had gone to bed. I was sitting on our grey three-seat sofa. It finally dawned on me that Jesus, through whom everything was created, after leaving His heavenly realms, entered into the time and space continuum. He was rejected and despised by those He was reaching out to and after being flogged and tortured, died a horrible death on a cross. He had done this for me. As I thought about this, my eyes welled up and I felt tears rolling down my cheek.

That was probably the moment I decided to become a Christian. Jesus dying so that I may live a life in a relationship with God was not something I could be passive about and walk away from. I simply had to react. My reaction was to give over my life to God and live according to the instruction in the Bible. On the 25th April 1992, at the Elephant & Castle swimming pool, I was baptised into Christ by Michael O'Hanlon. Ranald was there. Jean although reticent about the church also attended my baptism.

I recall that after my baptism we met together in a flat on Tower Hill. Michael prayed and I remember him praying "Lord I know Satan is hopping mad right now."

> "Lord I know Satan is hopping mad right now."

Later on, as years went by, when I became familiar with the hymn, *I Vow to You My Saviour*, and the verse, "Soul by Soul and silently his kingdom marches on", the words of this prayer took on a deeper meaning as I reflected on the spiritual battle the Church is engaged in, and how the Church of Christ is built soul by soul, just as a literal church building is constructed brick by brick.

On the very night I was baptised, I received a phone call from one of my former colleagues at the Capital Newspaper Group. He was off to a nightclub and wanted me to come along with him. Sensibly, I declined and explained to him that I had just been baptised and wanted to spend some time in reflection. After I put the phone down I thought, was a "hopping mad" Satan trying to trip me up already?

I was recently speaking with a brother from Church, Ben Whitworth. He reminded me that he was there, present at my baptism all those years ago. He also informed me that the Elephant and Castle swimming baths no longer exist. I joked with him that it had clearly already served the purpose it was meant for, notably being the venue for my baptism!

Due to my work in the City, I was in contact with mainly white middle-class city workers in what was then the *City Ministry*, set up by the Church of Christ to reach out to professional people. The atmosphere at home after my baptism was a little bit frosty as Jean thought I had been sucked into a strange cult. As a black family, we mainly had black friends. Suddenly Jean was at my baptism and we were surrounded with a new bunch of people most of whom were white. Not being one for half-measures, I naturally attended all the church meetings. So now not only did I have a new bunch of Christian friends, I was out of the home every Sunday and two evenings a week.

Some of our conversations became heated as Jean felt that she was losing me to the church. I remember on one occasion, sharing a passage with Jean from the Bible and discussing Jean's need for God. Jean responded by saying to me with stern poker face and pursed lips, *"I will never join that church."*

I remained faithful that Jean would have a change of heart and prayed regularly for her. Jean has very high standards and there where places I would go in my sin that Jean would never venture. Jean had caused roughneck Randal to raise his game even before I had become involved with the church. I remember the day I came to the realisation that Jean had a naïve trust in me that I would never be unfaithful to her.

To Jean it was very simple. I loved her therefore; I simply would not get involved with other women. She trusted me unquestioningly. The truth was very different. My view was, what Jean doesn't know cannot harm her. However just as I found myself unable to cause serious harm to Raj after he burgled my house, I found myself unable to continue in my casual "laissez-faire" attitude of being attracted to women; I developed a tremendous sense of having to raise my game to avoid crushing Jean's spirit by getting involved with other women.

Jean and I were married on 9th September 1989 at St John's Church in Hackney. After saying our marriage vows, I remember thinking I will never disrespect my marriage with unfaithfulness. Early on in our Christian walk, someone who was influential in our lives was John Partington, a full-time minister. Jean and I are very different, John referred to me as a lion. I think he was alluding to the crazy zealous side to me. Well, if I was the lion, I am pretty sure Jean was the lion tamer.

Eventually, after a few months had turned into the best part of a year, Jean realised that this new church life was not a passing phase for me and was something that I had fully embraced. Slowly, but surely, she started to warm to the idea of attending church with me. We even had a few meals with another couple in the church who lived at nearby Stamford Hill who had invited us into their home.

In 1993, a few months after Jordan's birth, the UK Church had a retreat at Keele University in Staffordshire. This was a chance to get away and mix some inspiring spiritual teaching with lots of fun activity. As a family, we had not had a holiday in several years. I sold the retreat to Jean on the basis that it would be a change of scenery, a bit of a holiday for the family. Reticent but open Jean agreed. So I packed my family into our small Austin Metro and we drove up north for the four-day conference.

When we arrived, we discovered that there had been a mix up with the accommodation. The couple organising the lodgings had assumed I was single, as they had never seen me with my family at church. When I turned up with my wife and three children, we were shown to a single room. Jean was not amused. She was determined to return home to London.

I reasoned that I was tired and it was possibly dangerous for us to drive all the way back on the same day with me so fatigued. I convinced Jean that we should go and get something to eat and then sleep and see how she felt about it in the morning.

Meanwhile, Michael O'Hanlon, who had studied the Bible with me and baptised me, managed to find us two adjoining rooms so Jean and I could have one room while our baby, Jordan, Keith and Alex shared the other room. The experience for them was excellent and the boys warmed to the change of scenery straight away.

In the morning after a lovely breakfast, Jean had softened somewhat and agreed that we would stay. I even persuaded her to join me in the first class of the day. It was the perfect class I thought to take her to. The title captured my attention straight away, *Become a Powerful Black Leader for God*.

As we entered the hall with possibly a hundred other men and women of Afro-Caribbean descent, I think any lingering notions on Jean's part that I had joined a white middle-class cult were erased for good. This conference was a turning point for Jean. She now had people within the church she recognised and with whom she felt comfortable.

After returning home, Jean kept in contact with those she had come know and started to study the Bible with Deirdre Babalolu and Debbie Loban. The studies went well and Jean began to see the need for her own relationship with God. On 30th August, bank holiday Monday, 1993, at the home of Steve and Barbara Gregory, our family Group Leaders at the time, I baptised Jean into Christ.

My wife who had twelve months earlier defiantly declared she would, "never join that church", had now become my *sister* in the faith. Jean has a favourite saying, "Never say never." In Jean's case, this comment was a self-fulfilling prophecy, and I smile when I think of it now.

> **My wife who had 12 months earlier defiantly declared that she would "never join that church," had now become my sister in the faith.**

Chapter Ten

Doubting, and Wrestling with God

"I believe, help me with my unbelief." Mark 9:24

The above words were spoken to Jesus by a desperate man. The unnamed man's words are immortalised in the narrative of the gospel of Mark. He had a son with serious mental health issues. It was believed the son was demon possessed and had been from childhood. The son was now a young man and serial self-harmer, a danger to himself. News of the healing miracles of Jesus was no doubt circulating around the villages and countryside.

The unnamed man did what I would have done if my own son had serious health problems. He took his ailing son along with him to meet the great healer. Then maybe just maybe his son would be rid of his demons. The account of what happened when he met Jesus has been documented in the ninth chapter of the gospel of Mark.

Mark lived at the same time as Jesus and was a disciple of Peter who was the probable chief source of Mark's information. Despite having enough faith to take the time out to journey to meet Jesus, despite hearing of all the great miracles of healing and exorcisms by Jesus, the unnamed man still struggled with unbelief. *"I believe help me with my unbelief."* This was the man's response to Jesus' admonition to him with the statement, *"everything is possible to him who believes."*

Peter would have heard these words exchanged and they no doubt resonated deeply with him. So deeply that he shared the incident with Mark who saw fit to include the words in his narrative. After all, Peter believed that Jesus was the Messiah but later struggled and left the fold for a time. He too, needed help with his own unbelief when his Master and Teacher was captured and imprisoned by the Jewish leaders.

Many non-Christians are like the unnamed man. There have been numerous occasions I have heard people say words to the effect of, "I believe in something. A greater force but not sure about the Bible and Jesus." Christians can be like this too. We can go to church, get fired up and excited and utter a loud *amen* to points made by the preacher. Then we can sometimes deny God's power in our lives with a faithless attitude to some mishap. Or, we read something in the Bible and struggle to accept it.

About one year into my Christian journey, I would say I suffered a crisis of faith. I was reading the Bible every day, praying every day, attending lots of meetings and sharing my faith with others. But far from being inspired by the Bible, I found myself reading the narrative and asking the question; Do I really believe all this stuff about Jesus silencing storms and walking on water?

However, God works in all situations and reveals Himself to us at the place where we are. He reached me again after I had drifted into a sea of doubt. This time it was through childbirth. Furthermore, He arranged it at a significant date in my life.

On Saturday 24th April 1993, my third son, Jordan, was born. I have been fortunate enough to have witnessed all three of my sons come into the world. Each occasion was a mountaintop moment that took me days to come down from. On the day of Jordan's birth, I remember seeing his tiny little head shaped like an egg coming out of my wife's womb. I could not take my eyes off this little person Jean and I had produced.

The fact that he was our third born son did not diminish the joy and excitement one iota. If anything for me the excitement was enhanced by the fact that we had a third son, had completed the triple crown of three sons back to back!

As I watched over our son, unable to take my protective and loving eyes off him, I recall seeing his egg-shaped head settle into a normal shape. Then it hit me, the miracle of childbirth is not just the conception and the fusing of two cells together to form one cell, with all the DNA material and coding for the development of another human being. What I also found amazing was the way a woman's body is designed to carry and develop the forming baby, then pushes the fully developed baby out of the womb through the involuntary contractions and breaking waters that precipitate the birth. The egg-shaped head and soft bones of the forming baby's skull are all about facilitating childbirth. This is clear evidence to me of design.

I think this crisis in faith ended there and was possibly the last time I ever doubted the existence of God. I have doubted myself, doubted my ability to remain faithful and doubted that God would work in my life. I also doubted that I would utter the words, *Jesus is Lord*, if it meant certain death at the hands of an evil despot. Following the birth of my third son, Jordan, who was twenty four at the time of writing, I have never again doubted God's existence. Sometime later, possibly years later, it occurred to me that Jordan was born exactly one year, to the day, after I was baptised. As a spiritual birthday present God has provided me with a third son. What are the odds of that happening? God determines times and places. As a police officer, I struggle to believe in coincidences.

> I think this crisis in faith ended there and was possibly the last time I ever doubted the existence of God.

To a certain extent, the law of the land backs up my philosophy. For example, if as a police officer I stop and search an individual, someone I know to be a gang member because I have formed the grounds that he looks suspicious and is up to no good. After searching him I then search the surrounding area and find a deadly weapon hidden under a bush, I would be inclined to seize the weapon and arrest the suspect for constructive possession of the weapon. As a suspicious police officer, I am not going to shrug my shoulders and say, "oh well, it is a mere coincidence that the deadly weapon was hidden under a bush a few yards from where I stopped him." Conversely, why should I then shrug off these significant events on dates significant to me, as mere coincidences?

It only increases my faith when I receive signposts such as these. I sometimes pray for guidance, and signs such as these, when I need to make important decisions. I have often in conversation with Jordan told him that I consider him my miracle child, and in the next section (Wrestling with God) I explain why.

I had experienced a similar epiphany in my character ten years earlier. Again, it was through childbirth. On this occasion, it concerned the birth of my first son, Keith.

As a teenager aged nineteen, I had been in a relationship with my girlfriend Jean for three years. Whilst at work, I received a phone call from Jean. It was on my office phone, as we did not have mobile phones in those days. Jean informed me that she was pregnant. At the time, I was not certain that I wanted to spend the rest of my life with Jean and my response was to swear. I was not ready for this! My own mother raised me along with my brother and sister single handed and lived a very sacrificial life.

I think it was the vivid recollection of seeing my mum struggle so hard to raise us that I had in my mind when I promised myself that I would never put the needs of the baby before my own needs. I was a selfish teenager!

> "You will harm my son over my own dead body."

However fast-forward nine months. I am holding Keith in my arms by Jean's bedside at Hackney Hospital, looking down at him. My position with regard to sacrificing for my baby son has changed. I am now saying to an imaginary foe, "You will harm my son over my own dead body." I connected instantly with my baby son. The second he came into the world, the very moment, I laid my eyes on him.

I believe that this connecting mechanism is common to men. This instinct is by design; it is how God made us. Here is some food for thought. If we are made in the image of God, then this connection may well be how He feels about us when we are born. On this note, I will close the section with the words of the psalmist who wrote;

> *For you created my inmost being;*
> *you knit me together in my mother's womb.*
> [14] *I praise you because I am fearfully and wonderfully made;*
> *your works are wonderful,*
> *I know that full well.*
>
> Psalm 139:1)

Wrestling with God.

> That night Jacob got up, took his two wives, his two female servants and his eleven sons, and crossed the ford of the Jabbok. [23] After he had sent them across the stream, he sent over all his possessions.
>
> [24] So Jacob was left alone, and a man wrestled with him till daybreak. [25] When the man saw that he could not overpower him, he touched the socket of Jacob's hip so that his hip was wrenched as he wrestled with the man. [26] Then the man said, 'Let me go, for it is daybreak.'
>
> But Jacob replied, 'I will not let you go unless you bless me.'
>
> [27] The man asked him, 'What is your name?'
>
> 'Jacob,' he answered.
>
> [28] Then the man said, 'Your name will no longer be Jacob, but Israel because you have struggled with God and with humans and have overcome.'
>
> Genesis 32:22

Six weeks after Jordan was born Jean and I came down from the mountain with a crash. During the pregnancy, Jean and I were both tested for a blood disorder, Sickle Cell anaemia. This is a dreadful disease caused by an abnormal blood protein, which renders red blood cells unable to maintain a conventional disc shape. The resulting deformed sickle-shaped cells can often clump together causing excruciating hellish pain as they get stuck in the small blood vessels known as capillaries. The pain is so intense that sufferers are routinely administered morphine to control it. When our blood test results came back we both found out that we were carriers of the disease and had what is called, Sickle Cell Trait.

The fact that I carried the disease was a bit of a shock to me. Sickle Cell is a disease that primarily afflicts black people and I am mixed race. As I am fifty per cent white, in my logic, my mother's white genes made it unlikely that I would be a Sickle Cell carrier.

Having discussed the options with the doctor, we were offered the opportunity to abort due to the risk of our son being born with this life limiting genetic condition. At the time, Jean was not a Christian and I was very young in the faith. However, it was never a viable option and we decided that we would press on with having the baby. Both our other sons, Keith and Alex, were also tested and neither was shown to have the disease. Perhaps this lulled me into a false sense of security.

I put the blood test Jordan had to the back of my mind and pressed on with my happy life still content in the knowledge that I now had three sons and life was going very well. However, I returned home from work one evening and as I entered our front room, Jean was on a chair, head held in her hands and crying. Concerned, I asked her what was wrong and through tearful eyes, she said, "it's Jordan!" The results had come back and he was shown to have the disease.

Doctors had said that if both parents are carriers there is a one-in-three chance that any children born to them would have the disease. Jordan was our third son. This news hit me real hard.

For the first time, I questioned God. What was he doing? Why had he allowed this to happen?

> I was angry with God and this was no model Lord's Prayer recited off by heart. This was me keeping it real

One evening shortly after receiving this devastating news, I remember I was alone in my car driving along and praying as I drove. I recall punching the steering wheel of my car and calling out to God in anguish "he, (Jordan) has already touched our lives!" The thought of losing him was just too painful for me to contemplate. I was angry with God and this was no model Lord's Prayer recited off by heart. This was me; keeping it real with God, getting angry and wrestling with my true feelings. Scripture tells us that God is close to the broken hearted. I honestly believe that God was close to me and at that moment, heard and saw everything and was moved to act.

As the weeks turned into months and months, into years, Jordan was perfectly normal, perfectly happy and in very good health. We had joined a local Sickle Cell

Support Group in Hackney and learned all we could about the illness and how to manage it. Jordan grew and showed no signs of the illness. Many of the other children with Sickle Cell however, where in and out of hospital every month.

The Hospital regularly took samples of Jordan's blood so that he could be monitored and due to this, the Sickle Cell Specialists had a comprehensive picture of how Jordan was developing and what was going on with his blood.

When Jordan was about eight years old and appearing so healthy without ever suffering a crisis, we questioned a consultant, asking why Jordan was not suffering like many of the other children with the condition. The consultant explained to us that baby blood is different to adult blood. He told us that typically, a baby would lose all the foetal blood by the age of two years. Jordan for some reason had retained an unusually high amount of his foetal blood and that this was having a prohibitive effect on his blood 'sickling'.

Naturally, Jean and I were greatly comforted by such wonderful news. I later reflected back to my desperate cries out to God after Jordan was diagnosed. God had heard me, simply flicked a genetic switch and Jordan was protected. It is for this very reason that I refer to Jordan as my miracle child. I took it to the Lord in prayer and He delivered big. Of course, Jordan's blood chemistry was different! I believe entirely that this was God's doing, a personal intervention by God in response to some very intense praying.

I remember sharing this with a brother, a mature leader in our church whose life is a work of service. However, I could tell from his body language that he didn't quite share my belief that this was God ordained, as he said ,'if that is what you want to believe that's fine." I must admit I was somewhat taken aback by this as the brother is a Church Leader who I would have expected to have a greater faith in the power of prayer to move God. However, I have absolutely no doubt.

If we do not believe God has worked when a prayer is answered, what is the point of praying? When consistent prayers are lifted up, amazing things can happen. Jesus promised the Holy Spirit until the end of time. Do we do God a disservice when we put healings and apparently answered prayer down to fate, coincidence or mere good fortune?

Jordan's unique blood composition does not totally preclude him from a sickle cell crisis. In 2003, aged nine, Jordan contracted a primary condition, salmonella food poisoning. The primary condition put Jordan's body under so much stress as it battled to rid itself of the food poisoning, it triggered a secondary response and Jordan went into a *blood-sickling crisis*. This was the first time Jordan had experienced a full-blown Sickle Cell Crisis and he had to be admitted into hospital where he remained for ten days. Jean and I took it in turns to stay with him at his bedside. I was still on probation with the Met Police so I was too scared to take any time off, worried that this would hinder me getting through the probation period. It was a tough ten days, getting very little sleep and completing my shifts before returning to hospital to relieve Jean and stay with Jordan.

He was on morphine doses and I thanked God that we lived in the Western world with an excellent health service to care for our son, and not some third world country without access to skilled medical attention. However, morphine is a very powerful drug and can only be used sparingly.

There were times when Jordan's pain began to break through again over an hour before he was due to take another dose. Those were long hours spent clock watching. Each minute Jordan had to wait before he could be given more morphine to quell the pain seemed to drag on endlessly. I can tell you that if I had £100,000 in life savings, and was given the choice of being able to pay to swap places with him and take the pain, I would have done so without hesitation and emptied my account.

I believe that we have to go through certain experiences in life before we can fully appreciate the sacrifice God, the Father, made in sending his own son to earth in order to go through pain and suffering for us. If I, a wicked man who only ten years earlier had promised himself never to put his child's needs before his own, was willing to make such a sacrifice and was feeling so much pain, how then must God, the perfect father, have felt about Jesus' suffering on the cross at the hands of men?

The whole experience of Jordan's suffering awakened me to the love of God like never before. As Christians, we take what we call the Lords Supper together. It is the most reverent part of our worship service. The event is usually accompanied by a short communion talk, which is geared towards helping worshippers focus on the cross of Christ and what it means for us today.

Without exception, the best communion talk I ever heard was by a brother named Iggy, at the Wembley Conference Centre at one or our big invitational services. Iggy preached the communion. His deep voice filled the auditorium as he shared from Mathew 27:45.

> [45] *From noon until three in the afternoon darkness came over all the land.* [46] *About three in the afternoon Jesus cried out in a loud voice, "Eli, Eli lema sabachthani?" (which means, "My God, my God, why have you forsaken me?")*
>
> [47] *When some of those standing there heard this, they said, "He's calling Elijah."*
>
> [48] *Immediately one of them ran and got a sponge. He filled it with wine vinegar, put it on a staff, and offered it to Jesus to drink.* [49] *The rest said, "Now leave him alone. Let's see if Elijah comes to save him."*
>
> [50] *And when Jesus had cried out again in a loud voice, he gave up his spirit.*

He preached the analogy that the darkness that came over the land while Jesus was suffering and dying a slow drawn out death on the cross of torture was indicative of God grieving over his own son, a visible outpouring of God's pain. I really identified with this analogy. My own heart was darkened by sorrow when I had to sit there helplessly seeing Jordan go through so much pain.

Prior to hearing Iggy share his communion talk, I had possibly overlooked the likelihood of God suffering pain, seeing Jesus on the cross. After all, He was God and He knew his plan to raise Jesus back to life. However, the fact remains that Jesus' suffering would have been hard for God to endure and this visible manifestation of grief (the darkness) was indeed indicative of this. It took my own experience of seeing my son suffer, for me to connect with God the Father's role and suffering during the crucifixion of Jesus.

Chapter Eleven

Answered Prayers and Inspiration from A Little Old Lady

"For the eyes of the Lord are on the righteous and his ears are attentive to their prayer..." (1 Peter 3:12)

If you hang around faithful praying people for long enough and you pray hard enough you will soon have reason to believe that prayers can be powerful and effective. I wrote earlier about how I wrestled with God in prayer after the devastating news of our third son being diagnosed with Sickle Cell disease. Jordan's normal and healthy life to date has been tremendously faith-building for me and I frequently thank God in prayer for this. I consider it to be a personalised present to me from a loving Father. Every single day Jordan spends in good health is a gift from God to me.

Over the years, there have been countless other examples of answered prayers that have had the effect of nurturing my faith. One powerful occurrence happened shortly after Jordan's diagnosis. At a gathering of our churches at Alexandra Palace, possibly the same one that I had been reticent about attending prior to being approached by the young man I had reached out to years before, the congregation was informed that Joseph Kanu, the child of Sam and Emily a married couple in our church in South East London, had been admitted to hospital with meningitis, the bacterial form which is often deadly.

By all accounts, the prognosis was grim and the expectation was that Joseph would not survive. Our speaker who announced this then led the congregation in a prayer for healing. I can vividly remember a sea of heads, possibly a thousand people, all bowed in corporate unity as our speaker prayed. Over the next few days and weeks, Joseph defied all the expectations of the medical professionals. He recovered;

our prayers for his survival and healing were answered.

Over the years my wife and I have become accustomed to speaking to the Kanu family at these gatherings and we always look out for them when we have our tri-yearly church-wide services in central London. In order to document accurately and emotively this wonderful faith-building episode I have interviewed my friend, Sam Kanu, in the same way I would, a witness in one of the cases I investigate and what follows is his statement of the event.

Sam Kanu Statement

My name is Sam Kanu. I was born and raised in Sierra Leone and have lived in the UK for twenty-seven years. I am married to Emily and we have three children. I work in the financial sector.

I write this statement about the time my eldest son, Joseph, survived a life threatening illness in 1996. These are the circumstances and details of what happened.

Joseph, our first born child, was aged ten at the time. He came home one afternoon after school and he complained of having an intense headache. We took him to see our GP, were advised to give him paracetamol and monitor his condition. The next day there had been no improvement in Joseph so we took him to the King George Hospital in South East London. Again, he was prescribed paracetamol and we returned home. However, that night Joseph collapsed at home, we called for an Ambulance and Joseph was rushed back to the King George Hospital. His condition rapidly deteriorated.

Over the next few days, as Joseph deteriorated further, he was admitted into the Intensive Care Unit (ICU) on the 14th December. This was when he was diagnosed with meningitis. We were told by the doctor that he was terribly unwell with only a 50/50 chance of survival.

However, we had faith. We were praying as a family and some of our church family were also praying for our son to pull through. We believed God would answer our prayers. When Joseph was taken ill, it was very difficult to cope because we had our two younger children, Sylvanus, and Samia, with us. They were very young. It was also very hard for them. We had to leave home early for work and stayed at the hospital most of the time after work with Joseph, whilst my mother-in-law looked after our other younger children.

We also received love and support from church members, especially from our local group with Helen and Remi Alaka, in particular, being a tremendous support to us. I have been asked by Randal if there was any particular scripture that comforted me during this trial. I would say the story of Job was a great comfort. He was faithful in his trials and God blessed his faithfulness. I recollect one night spent by Joseph's bedside at the hospital, reading through the book of Job.

After Joseph's condition deteriorated still further, doctors informed us that there was no chance of survival. The consultant informed Emily that keeping the life support machine on, was a waste of resources and that they would be turning the machine off and that we should prepare ourselves.

This conversation was on the Friday evening between my wife Emily and one of the Consultants. I was at work at the time. When I arrived at the hospital, Emily was very upset and tearful. After hearing from Emily what had been said about Joseph's chances of surviving, I went to look for the consultant. After about fifteen minutes, I found him in one of the corridors. I explained to him that we were Christians and had faith in the power of God. I stated that whilst there was one iota of life in my son, we would never give up on him.

On Sunday, we had a very big church service at Alexander Palace. Emily remained at the hospital with Joseph. I attended the meeting. I had notified the church leaders about Joseph's grave condition and asked for prayers. When the whole church prayed for our son and our family, my own faith was uplifted.

Alexander Palace is a very large venue and the meeting hall was very full. After hearing the prayer for Joseph, the whole congregation joined in and I believed that Joseph would survive despite what the doctors had already told us.

After the service I joined Emily by Joseph's bedside. We remained there throughout the night. On Monday morning, there was a queue of visitors from church. I recall that they formed an L-shape along the corridor and around the corner, as so many people had come to the hospital. One of the nurses asked if we were celebrities. I simply said no these people are from our church.

It was about 9:30am when the doctors and consultants were doing their rounds. We were in Joseph's room at the hospital in the ICU. The doctors met us inside the room. After a brief discussion between the three doctors, a professor, a consultant and a surgeon, they decided amongst themselves to remove the life support. They asked us to excuse them by waiting outside. The doctors were not confident Joseph would survive without the life support machine. Obviously, this news was devastating to hear, but we held faith in God.

We remained outside the door but we were able to see through the window. When they finally turned the machine off, they found that Joseph was breathing by himself. They called us back in and told us that Joseph is a fighter and they are ready to help him through this. They told us that even if he survives, his journey to recovery will be a slow and a long one. I recall that after the life-support machine had been switched off and Joseph kept on breathing by himself, the consultant said, "Your God is great."

This was the same person I spoke to in the corridor, told that we were Christians, and had faith. The same person I told that we would never give up if there was just one iota of life in our son.

About two or three days later, Emily and I were sitting by Joseph's bedside. Emily noticed some movement from Joseph's hand. Emily excitedly drew my attention to it. This was significant because he had been in a coma for about three weeks and during this period, there had been no movement whatsoever, not even a flicker from his eyelids. Joseph's return to consciousness was a gradual process. The finger twitches were followed by some movement of his toes. Within a couple of days, he looked at us. He was still heavily sedated. I recall the first words he spoke, "Mum and Dad".

During Joseph's illness I spent most of my time at the hospital. I was reaching out to other families with children in the ICU. The second week we were in the ICU, one of the children passed away. Three days after that another child passed away. This was probably my lowest point. For the first time I had doubts and wondered if Joseph would be the next child to die, but we held to the faith that God would pull him through. The young boy who died was twelve years old. I reached out to his parents and they only said, "thank you very much. Carry on believing in the god you believe in; we don't believe in God'.

Throughout the events of Joseph's illness in 1996, we were faithful in God and we firmly believe that God has been at work in Joseph's recovery up until today. We stayed faithful and never doubted in what God can do in his life.

[Statement ends]

There is a wonderful conclusion to this story. In January 2017, we had our first church-wide service of the year at Logan Hall in central London. As Jean and I were leaving the building, we bumped into the familiar friendly faces of Sam and Emily Kanu. As usual, we stopped for a quick chat and Sam introduced us to a young lady and a beautiful small baby. The lady was Joseph's wife and the baby their child, a son named Samuel. The doctors had given up all hope two decades ago and could only see a helpless dying child. God, however, had another plan and saw a future man, father and husband.

Jesus is a shepherd who looks after his flock. In fact, Jesus was so much into shepherding that he commanded his right hand man, Peter, to look after his sheep before he ascended into heaven after the resurrection. He also promised to send the Holy Spirit to be with his flock always until the very end of time. One incident that moves me when I think about it is something that happened over twenty years after I first met my sister in the faith, Siobhan O'Neil.

You may recall that whilst I was en route to my very first church meeting with the London Church of Christ, a woman approached me and invited me to church. I was having a serious touch of the *seconds* and was about to get off the train.

Siobhan, a complete stranger at the time, reached out to me, I remained on the train, and we journeyed the rest of the way together. I made it to church and within a few months made the decision to be baptised. Siobhan was always giving. She was very evangelistic. She was also a wonderful singer and songwriter. From time to time Siobhan would perform a solo at our church services in East London.

Over twenty years later, Siobhan was sitting all alone at a bus stop. She was undergoing chemotherapy having been diagnosed with lung cancer. She put up a brave and faithful fight but ultimately, she lost the battle and died very young, early into her forties. One afternoon I was alone, driving an unmarked police car, conducting some enquiries. I drove along Manor Road in Stratford, East London. I noticed Siobhan at the bus stop apparently lost in her thoughts head hung low. I stopped the car and called her name. She looked up and then as she recognised me she smiled. I asked her if she needed a lift. She got into the car and I drove her all the way to her home.

On the journey, she shared with me that she was on her way back from a hospital appointment and was feeling very weak. She shared how she had been reaching out to another cancer patient. This did not surprise me, as it was her character all over. However, feeling very weak from her exertions, she had just bowed her head and far from being lost in her thoughts, she had been praying. In her heart, she had cried out to the Lord in prayer, "this is so hard". It was at that point that she looked up. God had heard her prayer and had already made a provision. The first thing she saw was her Christian brother offering her a lift home.

I was deeply saddened when Siobhan died so young. She left a husband Mike, two young girls, both of whom I used to teach at Sunday school.

I frequently look at her oldest daughter when I see her at church and see Siobhan in her. I take some comfort in the knowledge that in her time of need on that one day when she felt too weak to manage, I was able to assist her. To me, there seems a wonderful and poetic return of her grace. The woman who reached out to me and encouraged me when I wanted to alight the train on route to salvation, was herself assisted in her own time of need. Siobhan, I have no doubt that having an instantly answered prayer when she was so low, would have had the effect of feeding her faith too.

My own walk with God has been seasoned with times when I have had a powerful sense that God has answered specific prayers and I find this very faith-building. Probably the quickest answer to a prayer I ever received was back in the 1990s. It was a period when our church was probably at its most mission focused in terms of encouraging members to bring friends to church. I had not had a friend attend church with me for a long while. Our family group leader at the time, Barry, was bringing all the visitors.

I remember feeling heavy hearted that I was letting God down and letting Barry down. So I went out to a solitary place to pray, early in the morning. I prayed specifically for a visitor. I wanted to be in the mission of helping to make disciples. I returned home and within five minutes, the telephone rang. I answered and a man named John asked for me. He wanted to know what time church service was that day, as I had invited him some time back and he had decided to take up my invitation.

There have been many times when God has blessed my finances unexpectedly. Numerous occasions where we have kept faith in difficult circumstances when finances were a worry and unexpectedly, we would receive money out of the blue.

One specific occasion happened in May 2016. Finances were a struggle. Jean was in poor health and had given up her job the previous summer. I had just taken my career break from the Met Police, and my net income had effectively reduced by at least a third. Furthermore, I was now self-employed so no work meant no money. We took the decision not to compromise our voluntary contribution to the church, so maintained our payments. Our church has a retreat for married couples each year and we decided to go as usual.

The cost was a bit of a burden financially but we both felt such times are too important to miss. The problem was it meant being away for the whole weekend and any taxi driver will tell you this is prime time to make money. I was also struggling with lots of headaches at the time and the fear was I would go out to work on Friday, over exert myself then get fatigued and be unwell with migraine for the *Marrieds Retreat*.

However, I was running scared. The comfort blanket of a regular income had gone and I decided I was going to go out early on Friday and earn £80 so that when we returned we would at least have some cash. This led to a bit of tension, as Jean was very familiar with the routine of Randal over exerting himself and suffering the consequences of a migraine attack.

So on the Friday morning, I mentioned to Jean that I would be going out for a few hours. Jean said, "It is ok, Randal you don't need to". I defended my corner and explained I felt I could earn £80 then at least be able to relax while we were away. Jean then insisted, "no Randal, it is OK you don't need to work today". She then handed me the envelope, which had arrived that same morning and said have a look. I pulled out the contents and saw that Jean had received a cheque from HMRC. It was a tax rebate for over £800. Suffice it to say, I relaxed myself and stayed at home until it was time to leave for the retreat, and a wonderful retreat and time of spiritual refreshing we had too. Free from worry and of course free from migraine.

When we had previously spoken about the retreat, we had prayed about it, even though by sight we could not see a way we could afford it. For sure, the money Jean received was owed to her and would have been paid anyway. However, the timing was for us a demonstration that God has us covered and we had an overwhelming sense that God had provided. God at work or mere coincidence, I will leave you to draw your own inferences on the timing of the arrival of the cheque.

An Evening With Hae Woo

Earlier I said that if you hang around faithful praying Christians long enough, you would soon have good reason to believe in the power of prayer. I recently met a wonderful woman whose faith in the power of prayer really acted as fertiliser for my own faith.

On Thursday 2nd August 2018, after a long day at work, I made my way from Romford Police Station to Central London. I had been invited by the charity, Open Doors, to meet a little old lady from North Korea, Hae Woo. Aged seventy and four foot eight not an inch taller by my estimation. Possibly the most remarkable Christian I have ever met personally. A few months earlier, my wife and I had made a donation to the charity. We received a letter of thanks for our partnership with them, and it was a few days after the letter when I received the phone call asking if I would like to attend the meeting.

"The most remarkable Christian I have ever met personally".

This was in March and August seemed such a long way off, so I did not hesitate to accept the invitation as it was not putting me under any immediate time pressures. However, time flew and before I knew it the 2nd of August was upon me. I was very busy, struggling with the unusually hot weather. The only thing that persuaded me to go to the meeting was that I did not want to go against my word.

Due to the nature of what Hae Woo is doing in speaking out against the tyranny of the North Korean Government where faith in anything other than the presidential deities or state run church, is not tolerated, Open Doors had to be very selective about who they invited to her talks whilst they were hosting her In the United Kingdom. In fact, I am not convinced that Hae Woo is her real name, I am assuming it is not, so that her true identity is protected. She still has family and friends in North Korea, and she certainly has planted Churches there; any one known to have associated with her would be guilty by association, and almost certainly persecuted.

As I walked through Westminster, past Parliament Square, I recall I was feeling a little unsettled. I had only informed Jean by text message earlier that I would be home late. Jean prefers I inform her in advance when breaking from routine. But instinctively I felt I had made the right choice even if executed poorly. When I arrived at the venue, there were a number of Open Doors staff members present, possibly five and maybe a dozen or so guests making an audience of around seventeen people in a small meeting room.

Hae Woo spoke via an interpreter. After an introduction, she shared her testimony in the form of an interview, the interviewer being Eddie Lyle, the President of Open Doors UK & Ireland. As I sat and listened, it quickly became apparent that I had made the right decision to attend. The extra effort to stay out and arrive home late was a good investment of my time. I was deeply moved by what she shared which I summarise for you now.

Hae Woo has been subjected to incarceration in the notorious Prison Camps of North Korea no less than ten times. As a child, Hae Woo remembers that her mother used to hold a cross on a chain and mumble to herself. She was taught when growing up in North Korea, that Christians were the worst people, wolves. Her mother never shared her faith with her children through fear that they would be sent to Prison Camps. However, her mother found her own way to express and live out her faith. She always shared what she had. People used to refer to Hae Woo's mother as a person who was born for other people. The first time Hae Woo came to know the words of Jesus was through her husband. He had been imprisoned. Her son visited him in prison and during the visit, her husband wrote on the hand of their son the following words.

"Believe in JESUS Christ and pray in his name that is the only way to survive in this land."

Hae Woo came to believe that her husband had found the truth. There was no happy ending for her husband. He was beaten and starved and when she visited him in the concentration camp, she did not recognise the emaciated man standing in front of her. It was the initiative of the prison guard who pointed out to her; look here is your husband. Her husband became a martyr and died whilst in prison.

Due to the persecution her family faced she escaped to China, which is a favoured refuge for many North Koreans fleeing for their lives. After escaping to China, Hae Woo found a church and was baptised. When asked if she has a favourite passage in the Bible she stated that her *go-to* verse is Psalm 23. It is the confession of her faith.

During the interview, Hae Woo spoke about a time after being tortured that she cried out and asked God for help. The voice of the Lord said to her, "think of the suffering of Christ on the cross." During her ongoing torture, she imagined images of Christ's life and became so focused on the images that she did not even feel the torture. When she was subsequently returned to her cell she heard God's voice say, "My beloved daughter, you walked through water today". I was intrigued by her choice of words and during the questions and answers session after her interview I asked her what was her understanding of God's words, "today you walked through water"

She answered that she was deeply moved by God's words and felt very humbled that God would pay her such a compliment; that she had walked on water.

I then understood what she meant. It appears that the walking through water was a mistranslation, what she had actually said was that she had heard God's voice saying, "Today you have walked *on* water." If God did say this to her then it is indeed a massive compliment. As far as I am aware the only documented occurrence of anyone walking on water is Jesus, and (briefly) Peter (Matthew 14:22), putting Hae Woo in a very elite group of three albeit metaphorically speaking!

Prison camps in North Korea are designed to break the will of those unfortunate enough to be there. The goal is to break the minds of the people there and 're-educate' them into the thinking of the state. Once, whilst being tortured, Hae Woo forgot herself. She was singing songs of praises as a distraction from the torture and actually started to sing too loudly so that the guards heard her. At times, her ordeal was so severe that she would cry out to the Lord in tears. On one occasion when entering into her tenth camp whilst praying, God spoke gently to her "Do not fear, I am here."

It is small a wonder that Hae Woo was so distraught at being in the camp. What she described to her small audience, was hell on Earth. Every day people would die of starvation or from injuries sustained from their hard labour. There were too many bodies so they were piled into heaps. Rats would eat away at the corpses. Those still standing would be forced to cut bodies into small pieces for cremation. In the midst of this hellish pit, a voice told her to sacrifice and share what she had. So she did. She would take her meagre ration and share her food with others. She would see momentary joy on the faces of people she shared her stale corn with.

Fuelled by this she decided to surrender to the promptings of God and risk her life by sharing her faith with fellow prisoners. However, she did not know how. To share openly would be to sign her own death warrant. God showed her who to talk to.

This is the verse she would share: "Believe in Jesus Christ and you and your household will be saved." (Acts 16:31)

She made an impact and ultimately, she converted four other women. They had a problem however, where would they meet together for worship. Such was the urgency to find a place as this was no doubt their joy and consolation, a platform to encourage one and other, God led Hae Woo to a toilet. A horrible stinky place used by nearly two hundred women. However, due to the terrible stench, it was the safest place as it was the one area the guards would not come near. So they would meet there for their worship.

After the Q&A session, Hae Woo was asked if there was anything that we as a group could be praying for, she gave us the following prayer list:

>To pray for the idol worship of North Korea to come to an end.
>For freedom of faith.
>For the people of North Korea to be able to go freely to churches.
>For God to protect the believers in the underground churches.
>For the reunification of North & South Korea.

As horrifying as Hae Woo's testimony was, it was also inspiring. One of the questions I have asked in this book is; why was it that the mighty Roman Empire could not eradicate Christianity from a small province it ruled? Well, to me Hae Woo's story is indicative of why. In a prison, a hopeless place of torture, a place bereft of compassion and any semblance of human rights, God used Hae Woo to start up a church of five women, bringing hope and igniting a small flame to spread the message of Jesus.

Hae Woo is a very serious looking woman. This after all that she has been through I can fully understand. She suffered from deep trauma and now still carried the mental scars. Having dealt with victims of abuse for many years now, I have come to understand that even in relatively low-level cases, the victims who report these incidents are left mentally scarred in some way, pretty much without exception this has been the case amongst those I have interviewed. There is nothing low-level about what Hae Woo has been subjected to.

My heart went out to her and I made sure I approached her and said goodbye personally before leaving. I felt somewhat insecure about giving her an embrace, not wanting to transgress any cultural divides that might offend, so I held her hand as I said goodbye. Whilst we held hands, she reached up and hugged me, so I kissed her on the cheek. The woman who ministered to other women in the labour camps of North Korea with a piece of stale corn, and news about Jesus, now ministered to me with a reassuring hug before I left.

Chapter Twelve

Bible Study: Food for Spiritual Growth.

Since my baptism in 1992 until the present day, my faith has grown considerably. Consistent Bible study has been the key to this growth. The Bible is the bedrock of the Christian faith. However, some people give up on the Bible too easily when confronted with some of the more difficult passages. They read something they find difficult to understand and rather than persevere they move on to another more encouraging verse. Certainly, this was my own practice for many years. I would read the Bible with a view to obtaining encouragement for my faith, revisiting familiar passages that I understood and found uplifting.

When I first started to read the Bible regularly, I kept on stumbling across amazingly encouraging verses. I called these little golden nuggets of encouragement and I think my early Bible study technique was based on trying to replicate these feelings of encouragement every time I sat down to read the Bible.

If I came across a passage that I did not understand, the temptation to move quickly on rather than get bogged down and expend energy trying to fathom things out, was a strong one. However, this is no longer the case for me. Even when reading some of the more *problematic* passages, I find that by following a few simple rules and asking specific questions around context, for instance, problems can be resolved. Such tenacity reaps a valuable reward as, each time I gain an understanding of a problematic passage, my confidence in the Bible grows.

One book that I have read which I found greatly useful in providing guidance on how to interpret the Bible correctly is How to Read the Bible for All its Worth, by Gordon D. Fee & Douglas Stuart.

What follows is a case study on how I examine a passage. The reason this has found a place in this book about how my faith has grown, is this: It is very faith-building to scrutinise and examine problematic passages and find that they stand up under close examination. Apparent contradictions, for instance, when context is applied, are no longer contradictions. Consequently, we can build our faith on sound reasoning, as opposed to a blind faith based on a book we do not really comprehend.

The Rich Man and Lazarus (*Luke 16:19*)
A case study in understanding scripture.

> "There was a rich man who was dressed in purple and fine linen and lived in luxury every day. [20] At his gate was laid a beggar named Lazarus, covered with sores [21] and longing to eat what fell from the rich man's table. Even the dogs came and licked his sores.
>
> [22] The time came when the beggar died and the angels carried him to Abraham's side. The rich man also died and was buried.
>
> [23] In Hades, where he was in torment, he looked up and saw Abraham far away, with Lazarus by his side. [24] So he called to him, 'Father Abraham, have pity on me and send Lazarus to dip the tip of his finger in water and cool my tongue, because I am in agony in this fire.'
>
> [25] "But Abraham replied, 'Son, remember that in your lifetime you received your good things, while Lazarus received bad things, but now he is comforted here and you are in agony. [26] And besides all this, between us and you a great chasm has been set in place, so that those who want to go from here to you cannot, nor can anyone cross over from there to us.'
>
> [27] "He answered, 'Then I beg you, father, send Lazarus to my family, [28] for I have five brothers. Let him warn them, so that they will not also come to this place of torment.'
>
> [29] "Abraham replied, 'They have Moses and the Prophets; let them listen to them.'
>
> [30] "'No, father Abraham,' he said, 'but if someone from the dead goes to them, they will repent.'
>
> [31] "He said to him, 'If they do not listen to Moses and the Prophets, they will not be convinced even if someone rises from the dead.'"

Many years ago, as a young Christian possibly only a few months old in the faith, I heard something preached that unsettled me. The preacher appeared to be saying that Hell was a place of eternal torment. I immediately had an issue with this, as it did not fit into my understanding of a loving God, and punishment that fits the crime. I just could not process how a few decades of sinning equated to an eternity of suffering in Hell.

To use an analogy from our criminal justice system, criminal sentencing, how would you feel if you knew someone who had been caught shoplifting and sentenced to twenty-five years imprisonment? A well-meaning sister in the faith, who I confided in, shared this passage with me as proof on the existence of a place of eternal torment.

What I will do now is utilise my digging tools (who, what, why, when, where, how) to throw some light as to what this text is demonstrating. Does it show that Jesus taught that there is a place called Hell where sinners are to suffer for eternity?

What sort of narrative are we reading?

The rich man and Lazarus parable is unique. It is a parable and it is the only parable in the Bible that actually names one of the characters. Other parables talk of a king, a farmer, a son etc. This parable speaks of a rich man and then breaks from the norm and names, Lazarus. The fact that Jesus names one of the characters being spoken of, is possibly confusing for some people who treat the text in a more literal sense.

How should we interpret the parable? Can we take parables literally? No, we cannot. Commands and historical records we take literally, but parables do not fall into either category. Jesus said elsewhere that the Kingdom of Heaven is like a treasure found buried in a field. So, if you are out digging and find gold treasure at the bottom of your garden, have you found God's Kingdom? Of course not.

Who was Jesus' target audience? Jesus was addressing a certain sect in Israel. They were the religious leaders called, Pharisees.

Where were the Pharisees on the *belief spectrum*? Unlike another group of devout believers in Israel, the Sadducees, the Pharisees believed in the afterlife and taught that the righteous went to be with father Abraham in God's paradise whereas the sinners go to Hell. They also believed that riches were a sign of God's blessings for the righteous, (the original prosperity gospel still prevalent today in some charismatic churches) and that poverty and infirmities such as being crippled were somehow linked to sin.

When did Jesus tell this? What is the background to this story? The Pharisees had been trying to trap Jesus with a series of difficult theological and legal questions. This can be understood from the other gospels, John in particular. The Pharisees had made up their minds that Jesus was not from God and wanted to get rid of him. They had admonished Jesus for openly healing a man on the Sabbath. They even committed what Jesus referred to as the unpardonable sin by attributing the healing miracles performed by Jesus to works of Satan.

How did Jesus teach and preach? Firstly, Jesus spoke in parables because parables enable the hearer to paint a mental picture. Have you heard the saying a picture speaks a thousand words? Secondly, Jesus used a language tailored for his audience. Jesus was a master preacher and teacher in this respect. To fishermen, he spoke of making them *fishers of men*. To farmers, he spoke of seeds and harvests. His hearers *got* him instantly.

How did Jesus construct this parable of the rich man and Lazarus? Jesus, knowing what the Pharisees believed, introduced three characters to whom they would immediately relate: the rich man, the poor sick man, named Lazarus, and Abraham, but shock horror, Jesus switched where the Pharisees in their worldview would have placed the characters. The rich man, indicative of the righteous, was in Hell. Poor Lazarus was with their father Abraham in the lap of luxury. Jesus was calling into question the core of the Pharisaic belief system.

Having used my digging tools to explore this passage, what conclusions can we make about what the passage aims to teach?

Since the text is a *story* and not a *history*, and we are dealing with fictional characters It is a risky strategy indeed to use the parable of the Rich man and Lazarus as proof of the existence of a place of eternal torment. The text is a parable shaped to challenge the worldview of a certain influential sect within the nation of Israel. One of the conclusions I personally gained from my own study of the passage, was an insight into the character of Jesus.

He was not one for pandering to the influential. He could have buttered up the Pharisees and complimented them on their high standard of personal hygiene and adherence to the rules. They were positively OCD when it came to ceremonial cleanliness and observance of the Ten Commandments.

Jesus was no people-pleaser, and He cut to the chase. Jesus was the original radical preacher who came out swinging with a story that would put the Pharisees in a bad light, raising those who were sneered upon (the poor needy and sick) to the very place the Pharisees would have expected themselves to be placed in the story. He spoke the truth and let the insults fly at Him afterward. I so wish I could be brave enough and bold enough to be more like this.

> **Jesus was the original radical preacher who came out *swinging***

We do need to be very careful when making decisions on what a text is saying. The word in verse 23, translated as *Hell* is the word for "in Hades". This is important because there are three words used in the Bible, which reference the place of the afterlife. These are *Hades, Tatarus* and *Gehenna*.

They all mean different things. *Gehenna* is the final abode of the people who die apart from God, the unsaved. The word is found twelve times in the New Testament. In eleven of these instances, it is Jesus Christ himself who uses the term. For this reason, there is a strong theological argument that Jesus taught of such a place and therefore the existence of Hell in the sense of the *Gehenna* idea.

Tartarus is a word introduced into the Bible by the apostle Peter (2 Peter 2:4) and it is a bit like *Gehenna* but is a place for fallen angels, not people. The word used by Jesus is the parable of the rich man and Lazarus is the Greek word, *Hades*.

Interestingly, Hades is the place for the spirits of the dead whether good or bad, a waiting place. Therefore, it can be argued with some validity that to translate the passage "in hell" is a weak translation and does not give the reader the full meaning of what Jesus was really teaching at the time.

Finally, I just want to make something clear. I am not proposing the idea of Hell is false in the sense that many believe it to be. Having sat on the fence for many years, I am leaning towards a belief that there is a *Hell*, in some shape or form. But before I venture to write on the subject more study and prayer is required.

It may raise a few eyebrows that for much of my twenty-eight years in the faith, I have remained undecided on the *hell* issue. My view is that what I believe about Hell, is not a salvation issue. It does not determine whether I will be accepted by God because it is a subjective topic. I concentrate more on how I live my life and practice my faith.

What I am arguing is that the Rich Man and Lazarus parable is unsuitable proof and has been used out of context by some to demonstrate that Jesus taught and, therefore believed, there to be such a *place of torment* after death. Any proof text, taken out of context, is a pretext, so we need to be careful how we handle the scriptures. *"Watch your life and doctrine closely. Persevere in them, because if you do, you will save both yourself and your hearers." (1 Timothy 4:16)*

David and Goliath

Another part of the Bible I have explored with *detective* eyes is the account in 1 Samuel 17 of David fighting the giant, Goliath. Is this nonsense or does the story make sense? This is one of the best-known narratives in the Bible. David the Shepherd boy slaying the feared warrior giant named Goliath.

Even if you are only vaguely acquainted with the Bible, most people will have heard the account. Many regard it as fiction, a legend nothing more than a story. I have often heard preachers refer to it as "the story of David and Goliath," and I cringe every time I hear this said. I think it sends out the wrong message, especially to our children, or those we try to convince of the Bible's validity as a historical narrative. These are not fables, these are not embellished legends, these are historical accounts that we read.

To set the scene, the location is the valley of Elah. The book is named after the prophet God used to set up the kingship of Israel, Saul being the first of a succession of Kings. Dated nine centuries before the birth of Jesus, Israel is still trying to consolidate its position in the Promised Land, they have just come through the period of the judges.

These judges include Othneil, the first one after Joshua, Deborah the Prophet, who slew an enemy King by driving a tent peg through his head while he slept, Samson, who probably needs no introduction and Gideon, a military leader.

The people of Israel at their own request to the prophet Samuel were now under the first of a long series of kings. The Philistines had become a deadly foe, a thorn in the nation's flesh. David has already been anointed by the prophet Samuel, but he is under cover, as Saul is still living and clinging on to power, jealously guarding his position as king. Later he grows to resent David for his success and popularity.

So we join the narrative with two large armies in a valley, facing the other. The feared Goliath is taunting and challenging the army of Israel to a man-on-man, one-on—one, and winner take all fight to the death.

Frozen in fear, no one from the ranks of Israel dares take up the challenge. This went on for forty days, the same old drill the same old taunts, the same old lack of response from the lines of Israel. It becomes so embarrassing that Saul promises the hand of his daughter in marriage and tax exemption, to anyone who defeated Goliath. Then, of course, David steps forward, outraged that a mere Philistine would dare to mock the army of the God of Israel, no matter how physically imposing,

The first question we need to ask is, where is this place? Does the Valley of Elah really exist? An important point to note is that the Valley of Elah does exist. It is a well-known location and I have printed off some great photos from *Google maps*. I have given presentations about the reliability of this narrative and I usually produce a couple of evidential exhibits for my audience. Firstly, a photograph from Google maps and secondly a stone which an old friend Paul Reidy, brought back from Israel for me, which I use as material evidence that it is a real place, a geographical location. The stone itself was picked up from the ground as Paul walked along the valley. People could if they wish, visit the scene of the battle (crime scene). So evidentially the location in the narrative is sound. It is important to be clear about this, not Narnia from the fictional, Lion, The Witch & The Wardrobe, or Middle Earth from the Lord of The Rings but the Valley of Elah; a geographical location.

David then descends from the hill down into the valley armed with a sling shot and five smooth stones. He walks towards Goliath who threatens to make David *food for the birds of the air*. What follows is the equivalent of a first round knockout in a much anticipated boxing match. David uses his sling to shoot a stone and makes a direct hit in the forehead of Goliath who is felled instantly without landing a single strike on his unlikely adversary.

Another good question is how tall Goliath was. Some may disregard the account due to the talk of giants, and perhaps in their minds they compartmentalise the narrative in the mental box for fiction and legends, along with Jack and the Bean Stalk with its "Fe Fi Fo Fum; I smell the blood of an English man."

The truth is we do not know for sure. He is placed somewhere between six foot nine inches to nine foot. Even if he was six foot nine that would have made him huge in biblical times. With his imposing armour and helmet which would no doubt have added more inches, the worst-case scenario would have put him close to seven foot tall. I have heard heavy weight boxers much smaller than this, around six foot six inches referred to as, "a giant of a man." So we need to be clear when we talk about the narrative, we are not reading about a man the size of a tree getting ready to trample David under foot.

How did David defeat Goliath so easily with a single shot of his sling?

PRACTICE! It was in the field as a shepherd that David would have honed his skill using a sling shot to chase away predators from his father's flock. A skilled sling shot practitioner can hit a moving target with great accuracy from a far distance. This throws some light on what eventually happens when David goes up against Goliath. David would have practiced his sling shot technique for hours, every day while out in the wilderness. He would have practiced until his arms, back and neck ached. He would have set up targets. This was not a random chance lucky shot.

When a slingshot is released there is an audible snap. This noise is the end of the sling breaking the sound barrier when released. This speed generates tremendous power, which is why the slingshot can be a devastating weapon if placed in the hands of someone who knows how to use it. Goliath would not have seen it coming.

The row of the Philistine army camped out on the valley hill, would have seen David swinging something and many possibly wondered what he was doing. They could possibly have heard the snap and, because of their location in a valley, where sound rebounds, they may have heard it a couple of times. Then they would have seen Goliath stop suddenly in his tracks, fall face first onto the ground...then stunned silence as their minds start to process what had just happened to their talisman.

Was the sling shot landing on the target a supernatural occurrence? Was God, himself, guiding the stone? I do not think so. God works in us and gives us gifts. I believe that one of the gifts God gave David was tremendous hand eye co-ordination. That is what God used to bring down Goliath. Had David been a tennis player, he would possibly have been in the Roger Federer bracket, an all time great!

It is not a coincidence that Roger Federer consistently lands his forehand strikes inches inside the base line; outside of the reach of his world-class opponents. He practices this stroke time and time again. He practices until his arm aches. his back aches, his neck aches, until he is sore from his exertions. David's hundreds of days of practice, year in, year out would have given him *Federer* type accuracy with the slingshot.

All of the sudden the account of David felling Goliath with a slingshot begins to look highly plausible. Not a Bible story! Bible history! Maybe God has programmed gifts and talents into our DNA too.

Check this verse out for a corroborative clue within scripture into the type of accuracy amongst slingshot specialists in the days of the Old Testament era:

> *Among all these soldiers there were seven hundred select troops who were left-handed, each of whom could sling a stone at a hair and not miss.*(Judges 20:16)

Having explored the account of David and Goliath, the narrative is something that makes perfect sense. The location is real and can be visited. David was a highly skilled practitioner of the slingshot. A weapon of war with which Goliath would possibly have been unfamiliar, used to fighting warriors with swords rather than shepherds with slings.

David that day was a man on a mission. He was focused and was not limited by his fear. Goliath, on the other hand, was so over-confident that he was insulted that Israel had sent a 'mere boy' to challenge him. The rest is history. I would go so far as to say this: Not only is the account of David slaying Goliath plausible, it was a mismatch. Due to David's focus and great skill with the slingshot, Goliath's over-confidence and facing an unfamiliar way of fighting, this was a perfect storm of circumstances. Goliath had no chance! He was doomed from the moment David collected the stones and loaded his sling.

> **David & Goliath was a mismatch Goliath had no chance!**

I can just imagine when David wrote Psalm 23 he was thinking about his fight with Goliath. The fight took place in the Valley of Elah. As he descended into the valley of death, *death* being Goliath with his enormous sword, angrily hurling insults, with his figure casting a huge shadow in the wilderness sun; a *shadow of death*, David might well have been reciting the words that later became immortalised as Psalm 23.

> ^{1}The Lord is my shepherd; I shall not want.
> ^{2}He makes me to lie down in green pastures;
> He leads me beside the still waters.
> ^{3}He restores my soul;
> He leads me in the paths of righteousness
> For His name's sake.
> ^{4}Yea, though I walk through the valley of the shadow of death,
> I will fear no evil; For You are with me;
> Your rod and Your staff, they comfort me.
> ^{5}You prepare a table before me in the presence of my enemies;
> You anoint my head with oil; My cup runs over.
> ^{6}Surely goodness and mercy shall follow me
> All the days of my life;
> And I will dwell in the house of the Lord Forever.

In summary, the Bible does have some passages that are difficult to understand,

and some accounts that we reduce to stories and legends in our psyche. However, by employing some common sense in our approach to studying problematic passages, and deploying some simple questions, we can gain a clearer and more accurate understanding of the text. Furthermore, we do not have to acquire a full understanding of every passage in order, to be right with God.

There are some very subjective issues such as the existence of Hell as a place of eternal punishment, and, even amongst *seasoned* Christians, opinions on some of these issues, often differ. The Bible also has narratives that are unfairly written off as stories, mere embellished legends. However, I have demonstrated that when the circumstances are examined, these so-called legendary stories, gain some serious credibility.

Chapter Thirteen

Sowing Seeds

Again Jesus began to teach at the lake. The crowd that gathered around him was so large that he got into a boat and sat in it out on the lake, while all the people were along the shore at the water's edge. [2] He taught them many things by parables, and in his teaching said:

[3] "Listen! A farmer went out to sow his seed. [4] As he was scattering the seed, some fell along the path, and the birds came and ate it up. [5] Some fell on rocky places, where it did not have much soil. It sprang up quickly, because the soil was shallow. [6] But when the sun came up, the plants were scorched, and they withered because they had no root. [7] Other seed fell among thorns, which grew up and choked the plants, so that they did not bear grain. [8] Still other seed fell on good soil. It came up, grew and produced a crop, some multiplying thirty, some sixty, some a hundred times."

[9] Then Jesus said, "Whoever has ears to hear, let them hear."

Mark 4:1-9

The Christian life should be a purpose-driven life where Christ-followers busy themselves in the field sharing the good news about the provision Jesus has made available for salvation, a pathway to a relationship with God for all sinners. For many years from childhood, all the way through to my adult years, I spent countless hours, day dreaming about being a world-class sports personality, an all-conquering sporting hero. In my mind's-eye, I lifted the FA Cup. In my minds-eye, I had my hand lifted in victory after fighting for the world light heavyweight title. In my minds-eye, I was first past the post in the Olympic 100 metres final. I received fame and adulation. I would replay these imaginary events in my head many times.

These days, as I negotiate my middle-age years, I am under no illusions that I am going to be a superstar. I have been released from my cage of self-focused daydreaming. A wonderful bi-product of this captive being set free of such self-centred thinking is I now spend time dreaming big for Christ. I dream of changing a destiny, of grabbing a lost soul out of the fire of this world that has drifted away from the safety of God's standard.

The small seed of faith that was planted in me twenty-eight years ago has grown to the extent of bearing fruit and now is striving to sow seeds of faith in others. This has become my primary focus in what is now a purpose-driven life.

Faith Sharing Confessions of a Taxi Driver

In April 2016, I decided to take a career break. I had been suffering the effects of stress due to the sheer volume of work and the intensity of some of the cases with which I had become involved. The straw that broke the camel's back was when towards the end of 2015, Jean was diagnosed with a serious illness called Amyloidosis. Life expectancy without treatment is one or two years and the only treatment available to her was chemotherapy. At one point, Jean was so weak that she became highly dependent upon me on a daily basis for care and help.

Juggling such a demanding job and meeting Jean's care needs was too much for me and my own health began to suffer.

To support my family during my time away from police work I qualified as a local taxi driver in Basildon. This was the perfect job for me as I was completely in control, of my hours and could make all Jean's hospital appointments. I could meet Jean's care needs, offer emotional support and make sure she was comfortable before I went out to earn some money. For this reason, I tended to do evening and night shifts. Furthermore, if Jean was having a bad day I would stay with her. If my chronic migraines were playing up, I no longer had to take strong prescription painkillers just to get out of the door and into the office. Going to work with so much medication in my system often left me struggling to take things in and concentrate.

A major positive that developed in my life as I took a career break, was plenty of opportunities to share my faith and reach out to people. In the taxi, I had a captive audience for the duration of the journey. I recall one airport trip where I spent much of the time on the journey sharing about Jesus to the businesswoman I had picked up from Heathrow airport. She was also a Muslim. I made sure I spoke up about what a radical man of God Jesus was, and how Mohammed in the Koran encouraged that all scripture should be respected, even the words of the followers of the way (Christian scripture). God opened up for me a tremendous channel for faith sharing.

As a taxi driver, I was presented with some wonderful opportunities to strike up God conversations. The early seeds of faith planted in me through my interactions with Ray Tom, Ranald McDonald, and the Tottenham Court Road platform preacher, it could be said, fell on good soil and the Word planted in me has multiplied. I now strive to lead a purpose-driven life geared at sowing the Word.

I recently watched a film called, *God is not Dead*. In the film, one of the main characters is a respected university Professor of Philosophy, who came from a religious background but has since become an atheist. He had developed a hatred of religion and tried to humiliate and undermine a Christian student who dared to take him on in a debate about the existence of God. The film has a tragic ending for the professor who is killed in a car accident.

However, the tragedy has a wonderful twist as God arranges for a Christian minister to be at the exact spot where the professor meets his end. The minister reaches out to the dying man and ministers the Word to him. The professor finally accepts and acknowledges God. The point that resonated with me was that God saw past all the vindictiveness the professor had showed towards the young Christian student. He saw past all the intolerance the professor had towards believers and gave him a final chance of redemption before his last and dying breath.

One conversation in the taxi that springs to mind is the one I had with a feeble-looking old man who, I guess, was in his eighties. If he was younger, he must have had a hard life. When I collected the old man, it took him a good while to shuffle his way up to and then into my car. If ever I saw a man coming to the end of a long life, this was him; he cut a pitiful figure. During the short journey to his home, as we spoke, it became apparent that this feeble old man still had some fire in his belly. We spoke about boxing and he proudly proclaimed that he was not impressed with boxers wearing gloves, real men were bare fisted. The conversation continued and he mentioned he would gladly use a knife and stab someone in the eye. I asked him why he hated so much and if he believed in God. His response was defiant. He swore in reference to the Jewish God and asked, "Where was He when they torched all the Jews in the gas chambers?"

I paused for thought, momentarily stumped by his question. After all, he did have a point, where was God when the Jews were being herded like cattle into the gas chambers? I contemplated how I could reach out to someone so filled with hatred and anger; so closed to God.

I try to rely on the Holy Spirit in these situations and hoped that He would give me the words to say. Clearly, I had no chance on a five-minute taxi ride of converting an eighty-year old man full of such anger. However, perhaps I could plant a seed. I informed my passenger that I felt he was a bit sparky so that is my nickname for him. As I pulled up to his destination, I said to *Old Sparky* that I had a message for him. He listened to me as I informed him that the Jewish God sent his son to die for all those sent to the gas chambers, and the Jewish God had sent his son to die for him too. After saying this, I got out of my taxi and assisted *Old Sparky* to his front door.

Nothing more was said. But I tried to be like Jesus and meet the physical need rather than just preach. As I drove off and contemplated our conversation, I wondered how much longer *Old Sparky* had to live. I replayed how disrespectfully he spoke about my God. My eyes welled up, not because he had insulted the God, I worship; God is big enough to take insults from feeble humans on the chin unruffled, but what ignited the emotion in me, as I said a prayer for the old man, was the fact that God had sent to hate-filled *Old Sparky*, a Christian taxi driver in, perhaps, a desperate attempt to reach out to him. Maybe one last attempt before they meet.

I remembered the film about the philosophy professor who hated religion, and how God never gives up on people. It reminded me that God's grace is a wonderful thing. In my minds-eye, I see *Old Sparky* on his deathbed, weeping. Not with sorrow that he is about to die, but with tears of joy as he realises that the Jewish God was not passive as people suffered.

The God of the Jews sent his only son into the world for their salvation. As angry Old Sparky contemplates that God extends salvation to all who repent of their sins and believe in Jesus, tears roll down his cheek, he prays a prayer for forgiveness and his face lights up with joy before he exhales his final breath and his life leaves his body.

The final passage from the Bible that he read, was the account of the thief on the cross who the dying Jesus assured had a place in God's Kingdom! I recently picked up *Old Sparky* again for the same journey. Disappointingly, he showed no signs of softening and was as angry and defiant as ever. However, I am still daydreaming about his conversion.

On another occasion, I picked up a woman who was visiting from Ireland. Her brother was in a hospice so she was spending some time with him, staying at his flat at night and visiting him during the day. We got talking and she informed me she was a Catholic and had a strong belief in God. She said this with some confidence. She told me that she felt like God had been sending her lots of messages. So, I asked her what form these messages had taken. She told me that everywhere she went, she keeps seeing the word 'hope'.

I probed a bit deeper into her faith. I discovered that she had long since stopped attending church and that she did not even read the Bible. However, she did say that she thought her brother had a Bible in the flat. I reasoned with her that God's Word was to the soul as oxygen is to the lungs. Spiritually you just cannot survive without it.

By the time we reached her destination, her self-assuredness had been replaced with a look of concern. Before she exited my taxi, she asked me, "Where should I begin?"

I simply said, "The Gospel of Mark. It is only sixteen chapters. You can read it in one night and it will tell you everything you need to know about Jesus, His purpose and mission." I sounded urgent about this. As she got out of the car, I bid her farewell and said again, "make sure you read it tonight".

Sometimes I have it in me to be quite pushy so far as encouraging people to read the Bible is concerned and I make no apologies for it. Imagine if that very night, she did exactly that. Imagine that she picked up the Bible, read the gospel of Mark and embarked on the road to a saving faith!

Thoughts like these inspire me to encourage the reading of Mark's Gospel. This is my *go-to* gospel for sharing about Jesus. It is the shortest of the four gospels, only sixteen chapters, compared to Luke, which has twenty-four and Matthew, which has twenty-eight. It cuts to the chase and really demonstrates the power and the dynamism of Jesus ministry and teaching.

I recently had the privilege of preaching in the Basildon Church of Christ. My sermon was based on Mark 5:21, which details Jesus healing a sick woman and then restoring life to a dead girl. Whilst I was preparing the message, an idea popped into my head that I found really inspiring. There is good evidence that the gospel of Mark was written by John Mark who was a cousin to Barnabas, a key member of the First Century Church in Jerusalem working closely with the Apostle Peter. Mark acted as an interpreter for him.

Police officers who regularly use interpreters when interviewing foreign suspects and witnesses will understand the close working relationship that develops with the interpreters regularly used. No doubt, John Mark and Peter the Apostle who shared the same faith and worshipped the same God, were very close indeed.

Peter, the rock, was Jesus' right hand man and was a key person in the building of the early church. Jesus knew that Satan would come after Peter and warned him of this. So, when Peter was executed and no gospel of Peter had been written, you could say that this was a good day's work for Satan. However, God always has a backup plan. If plan A fails there is always a plan B all the way through to plan Z.

There is written testimony from the early church that John Mark wrote down from memory all the things that Peter preached. Thus, when we read the gospel of Mark, we are really reading the words of the Apostle, the gospel according to Peter.

A few months ago, I was walking my dog in the Memorial Park in Wickford. I came across a man sitting alone on a bench. Thinking he was open to reflection, I decided that I should reach out to him. I said hello and made some small talk. The momentary pause before striking up a God conversation was long enough to make it awkward so I started on my way without sharing my faith. However, as I attempted to move away I simply could not do so. I do not know if it was my conscience, the Holy

Spirit or both.

The fact is, I was unable to move off without striking up a God conversation. Not knowing what to say, I vaguely remembered that the **Bible** says somewhere, *The Holy Spirit will tell you what to say*. So, I simply said, "Who do you seek?"

The man replied; "it is not who it is more what?"

He then went on to explain to me that he had been made redundant six months previously and just could not get a job having worked all his life. What he was seeking was a job. I asked him if he had any faith. He said no but stated if he got a job he might start to believe. I explained that I was a Christian and perhaps I had sufficient faith for the two of us. I asked for permission to pray for him right there and then.

> I asked for permission to pray for him right there and then.

Permission was granted; I prayed for him to find work and purpose. When I stopped praying, he informed me that if God answered that prayer he might start believing. I imagine the scenario that within a day or two he receives a phone call or a letter offering him employment. I imagine a scenario where I was able to plant a seed of faith that day. A scenario in which he gets the job, remembers our conversation and becomes open to seeking God, attending church and examining the scriptures. For sure, I am a dreamer, and I take great inspiration from the verse, which states that God is able to achieve immeasurably more that we can imagine. (Ephesians 3:20)

The truth is I have absolutely no idea if my conversations with any of these people have had or will have an impact on their lives. The scripture which opens this chapter makes it plain and clear that some seed falls on areas where it will not flourish. However, scripture also says, in a very matter of fact way, that some seed will fall on good soil and bear a crop of ten, twenty and a hundred fold.

I have a real conviction that if I persist in being in the mix with God, sharing my faith sowing seeds by striking up God conversations and conducting myself in such a way as to honour Jesus with the way I live my life, some of what I share will fall into good hearts, amongst people open to God and to change. Some will go on to do great things for God I am sure. It is not my business to know the details. It is simply my business to sow the seeds of faith, by sharing the word of God.

In summary, a small seed of faith was planted in me many years ago. Those disciples who planted the seed through their reaching out to me had no idea at the time whether I would be receptive to the Word or open to the faith. The parable of the sower reveals ahead of time that some seed will fall on good soil producing multiple crops. Twenty-eight years after my baptism, I am still attempting to sow seeds for God by sharing his Word with those I come into contact with. I have replaced my glory dreams with dreams of salvation for others.

Closing statement

During my service as a Police Detective, I attended court numerous times and became very accustomed to the trial protocols and what happens after all the evidence has been given. It became my custom to stay on at court after my work as *Officer In The Case* was done, and observe the closing of each case once all the evidence had been presented and all the witnesses had been heard.

Firstly, the Crown Prosecution lawyer will sum up the case against the accused, putting emphasis on the key points that strengthen the Prosecution's case.

Secondly, the Defence counsel will sum up the defence and identify any deficiencies in the Prosecution's case.

Finally, the Judge will give a detailed summing up and offer direction to the Jury before dismissing them so that they can deliberate and arrive at a verdict.

What I intend to do now is sum up the grounds and basis for the Christian faith. Once I have done this, you then get to be the Jury. You then get to decide for yourselves, having considered my personal testimony and all the evidence I have outlined, whether Christianity is an evidence-based faith, and therefore credible, or not.

Christianity has a long history of having to defend itself against overt attack. At various times and in numerous geographical locations, Christians have been slaughtered simply for being Christians. Even today, in our modern era there are many places where it is dangerous, to the point of being life threatening, to practice the Christian faith.

The charity, Open Doors, places North Korea at the very top of the list of danger zones. The attacks are not confined to physical. The core beliefs and doctrines of Christianity are always under scrutiny from sceptics. Despite these circumstances, Christianity has flourished like no other religion and has risen out of the shadow of the Roman Empire, which tried to destroy it, to become the world's number one religion. This fact in itself is remarkable.

In the West, the attack on Christianity is far more covert, and in the grand scheme of things, is more damaging. The core doctrines central to biblical faith such as the sanctity of marriage and adherence to God's plan of one-man-and-one-woman marriage is frowned upon and labelled as backward. When believers speak up for their beliefs, many have faced demotion or dismissal from their jobs.

The notion of creation rather than scientifically measurable evolution, has been dismissed as farfetched and naive. Common knowledge and popular thinking have clouded critical thinking and inhibited people from exploring the evidence in the first place under the misguided notion that science has all the answers. There is of course one slight problem with evolution. It is not scientifically measurable! For instance, if evolution were true, one would expect to find traces of the in-between species in the fossil records. Quite simply, they are not there.

I explored the evidence for Christianity in part one and then gave my own testimony of the transformation in my character as the initial basis for my faith. I had to make changes in lifestyle, a U-turn in where I was going, the decisions I was making. What I described was a *metanoia*, a word borrowed from the Koine Greek language the New Testament was originally written in. It is this tendency to transform the lives of those who read and embrace the teachings of the New Testament that is demonstrative of the power of what claims to be the Word of God.

I also spoke about answered prayers and how faith shaping life experiences can nurture a small seed of faith into something that grows into a purpose driven life; sowing seeds of faith in others. I presented the personal testimony of my friend, Sam Kanu, whose faith in the midst of adversity was an upward calling to me.

The recovery of Joseph, his son, was also faith building and set the tone for my attitude towards the need for corporate prayers, and for engaging in personal prayers with faithful expectation that God will respond and work things out for the best and in accordance with His will.

However, whether answered prayers are mere coincidences of good fortune or the miraculous workings of God is always going to be subjective so I spent little time talking about such things. However, in Part One I introduced evidence.

Evidence for faith is in abundance. Not wishy-washy weak ideas, but real credible reasons offering a firm basis for evidence based faith. It is only criminal law that demands proof beyond a reasonable doubt. Civil law is less demanding and will rule on a case on the balance of probability. I would argue that the evidence for the resurrection is proven beyond reasonable doubt due to the sheer volume of circumstantial evidence pointing towards the central doctrine of Christianity. However, as we live in the realms of the scientific era, and a man being raised from death to life is outside the quantifiable or measurable jurisdiction of set parameters, I would concede that there is always room for doubt.

For this reason, I rest my argument at the point of proven on the balance of probabilities. Such is the evidence; I will retreat no further. Pause for thought though. That means the resurrection of Jesus is more likely to have happened than not! The challenge for every sceptic then is to justify the rejection of an incident more likely to have happened than not.

I have demonstrated that the Bible makes sense when common sense and a few simple contextual questions are applied to problematic verses. I have demonstrated that Jesus was an historical figure; of that, there is no doubt, certainly not a myth. We explored the possibilities open to us. It is clearly apparent, that Jesus was no mad man. He was no liar for to lie gained Him nothing and the truth sealed His fate when He was rejected by men. So, the most sensible and logical option left open to us is that He spoke the truth and is who He says He is, the Lord.

I further demonstrated that the Bible displays a supernatural prophetic trait in that it contains history written in advance. It predicted for example the rise and fall of the Medo-Persian Empire and the clash of that Empire, with the Greek Empire under Alexander the Great. The Bible even details the sequence of conquests of the former empire as well as the number of divisions of Alexander the Great's Empire after he died suddenly in his prime. This premature death was also correctly predicted.

I also showed that the New Testament manuscripts, the very documents that Christians base their faith on, are about as credible as it can get when it comes to textual analysis. They were written early in the history of the church thus are deeply rooted with the Apostles. There are so many manuscripts in existence that comparisons are frequent and it is easy to identify any anomalies.

Simply put, discrepancies are nominal. Critics arguing to the contrary simply have not researched thoroughly enough. I have clearly exposed the evidence for Christianity as not merely confined to the Bible. There are extra-biblical sources from secular historians such as Josephus and Africanus. There is an abundance of attestation from key writers in the first and second centuries who all quote the scriptures, which make up our New Testament.

To slightly digress; for the purposes of this book, I have not introduced the arguments for the reliability of the Old Testament. Had I done so, I would have been introducing a chapter on the archaeological evidence available to us, and possibly another chapter on the Dead Sea Scrolls, which are widely regarded as the archaeological find of the twentieth century. The evidence in this field alone is extremely compelling in corroborating the Bible. Simply put, archaeological finds have always supported the historical narrative of the Old Testament. There has never been a find in history that has called into question historical facts detailed in the Old Testament, and survived further scrutiny from the top historical and biblical scholars.

Finally, if the above corroboration is not quite enough, I demonstrated that the single most important event in Christianity, the resurrection has compelling evidence to support that it occurred. There is even an extra-biblical account of the *great darkness* that came over the land whilst Jesus was dying on the cross. Christianity is not a simple *hope based on blind faith*; it is so much more credible than that. The Christian faith is no leap into the dark because of being blindfolded; it is more akin to a step into the light once the evidence has been considered.

There is compelling evidence around the circumstances surrounding the resurrection accounts. Potentially five hundred eyewitnesses, a missing body, lack of motive to create a hoax, the experience of those in key roles such as the guards, the recording of minor details in the gospels such as the folding of the burial cloths, the inexplicable conversion of Saul who hated Christianity and had set out to eradicate it from the face of the earth and the use of women key witnesses when a female would not be considered as a credible witness.

To reiterate, Christianity is an evidence-based faith. Wouldn't it be absolutely wonderful if a Christian apologist were able to call as a witness a legal professional at the very top of the tree so far as reputation and success were concerned? Wouldn't it be absolutely compelling if that top professional would then give testimony that the evidence around the key tenet of Christianity, the resurrection Jesus Christ, is reliable and trustworthy? Well it may surprise you that such a noteworthy witness has given just such testimony.

The witness I refer to, is none other than the eminent criminal defence lawyer, Sir Lionel Luckoo. If you look into the Guinness Book of World Records under the heading of the 'world's most successful lawyer', his name will appear. He came into the public eye for his remarkable achievement of two hundred and forty-five successful defences on murder charges. In an occupation where the stakes are at their highest, pressure at its greatest in the legal profession, he examined the evidence against his clients, and on two hundred and forty-five back to back trials, he exposed holes in the prosecution case and got his clients acquitted. This same tenacious defence lawyer has thoroughly reviewed the available evidence around the resurrection, and determined that the evidence is bereft of holes and can be relied upon.

After spending years studying the historical evidence around the central moment in the Christian faith, Sir Lionel Luckoo came to the following conclusion:

> " I say unequivocally that the resurrection of Jesus Christ is so overwhelming that it compels acceptance by proof which leaves absolutely no room for doubt"

The significance of Sir Luckoo's determination must not be understated. In order for a lawyer to perform in the elite arena of a murder prosecution, and achieve so much success, that lawyer must have remarkable analytical powers. He must know what constitutes reliable evidence better than anyone does. These requirements can rightfully be attributed to Sir Lionel Luckoo, twice knighted by Her Majesty, Queen Elizabeth. He became a noted diplomat and a member of the highest court in his country, Guyana.

The question I will leave the believer with is this: what are you doing to nurture your faith?

Members of the Christian faith need to become competent in expressing these facts to an increasingly sceptical world. It is my growing conviction that we need to invest an increasing amount of our time in studying God's Word so that we handle it with authority, and examine the arguments put forward by non-believers so that we can handle objections; exposing misconceptions.

To the sceptic my question is How much evidence do you need?

If after considering the evidence, you agree it is compelling, but still are unwilling to accept that there is a loving God who sent Jesus into the world to reconcile Himself to humanity, then perhaps your issue with the Bible is not an intellectual one at all, but an issue of the heart.

One of the most impacting scriptures in the New Testament is Hebrews Chapter 4:12-13, which I have previously referenced.

> *"For the word of God is living and active, sharper than any double edged sword, it penetrates even to deciding soul and spirit joints and marrow, it judges the thoughts and attitudes of the heart. Everything is uncovered and laid bare before the eyes of him to whom we must give an account".*

To paraphrase, you cannot hide a single thing from God, not a thing. A man can fool all the people most of the time, or most of the people all of the time, but he will never fool God any of the time.

About a year before my retirement from the police, I interviewed a detainee. It was shortly before Christmas. It was a case of domestic violence. The subject had turned up late at night to the home of his baby's mother. They lived separately. Their baby was a few months old. His partner had remonstrated with him as he had turned up drunk. He proceeded to beat her up grabbing her face, forcing her into furniture.

It was a sustained assault in which she received bruising on her lower back, arms and a bloody ear where her earring had been ripped out. Before an interview, we always check if, and for what, the detainee is known. In this situation my subject was well known for violence, this information was to prove useful to me in the interview. Likewise, God is aware of what we are known for and, furthermore, He knows our motives.

During the interview my subject presented a picture of someone who was contrite, someone who was himself a victim, he hated domestic violence as he witnessed his dad beat up his mother as a child. He added tears to his account and pleaded that he could not remember a single detail about assaulting his partner. He had been out drinking and someone must have spiked his drink! I have been around the block too many times dealing with suspects in interview to be sucked into these shows of contrition.

What I have tended to do is give them as long as they like to speak then once they run out of steam I start introducing the facts. He claimed that he was not a violent man and it just wasn't him. I introduced photographs of the victim's injuries and reminded him that this was the result of his actions a mere twelve hours ago, and said, "so it is you".

He fell back on the "someone must have spiked my drink" defence. I then introduced his bad character and reminded him that he had a previous conviction for assault and battery for which he had served a custodial sentence.

With each excuse and protestation I introduced another element of the bad character from his Police record. He again protested that he loved his girlfriend and was a changed man since she had met him when he was in prison and rescued him from that sort of life (drug use and violence). I then introduced an element from her statement that appeared suggest that this was not an isolated incident.

Finally he flipped, the spotlight on him had exposed the truth. The devil was in the detail. He started swearing, got up from his seat insisting the interview was over, and demanded to be returned to his cell.

My point is a simple one. I was an average run of the mill detective, but I was not fooled by the fake tears and words of contrition. People have absolutely no chance of fooling God. He sent His only son to die and give us all a free pass. One day we will all have to give an account to God for our decisions, including our decision not to follow Christ the saviour. If you the reader are not following, what reason will you give?

The stakes are too high and the costs of our free pass to salvation far too expensive to allow for sitting on the fence. We need to all make our own decision based on the evidence put before us.

I will conclude with the words of the Apostle Paul spoken after a protracted period of house arrest in Rome, defending his Christian beliefs before King Agrippa, and sharing about the resurrection of Jesus

> "What I am saying is true and reasonable." (Acts 26:25)

Choose for yourselves, but my contention is that Christianity is an evidence based faith, and were I to take the world to court on the charge of wrongfully insisting otherwise, I would have a strong case, there are far too many holes in the case against Christianity and the evidence in favour is very compelling.

Case Notes

I have striven to present the reason and grounds for my own personal faith evidentially. When I work on a case, I will accumulate a lot of information. What finally ends up used in court is often just the tip if the Iceberg. The information presented at a trial is my used material; this is the tip. However, there will be a great deal of information that is not relevant to the issues in question; this is the Iceberg that no one will see. This information has been retained as my unused material. Effectively what follows is my bibliography and recommended reading. I have also included one or two comments and items that did not make their way into the narrative of the book, as I did not deem them relevant to the main thrust of the case for my faith.

Bibliography & Recommended Reading

1. <u>Evidence for Truth Archaeology</u>, volume 2, Dr E. K. Victor Pearce

    The amount, of archaeological findings that support the Bible is extremely reassuring. I have not referred to this in my narrative as archaeology and the Bible have a tendency towards confirmation of the Old Testament which is not the focus of this book. However, in this book Dr Pearce strays off point a little as he explores the circumstances around the resurrection of Jesus. I found his insights and presentation of the facts very helpful.

2. <u>Christianity on Trial</u>, W. Mark Lanier, IVP Books.

    A Lawyer examines the Christian Faith. He presents Christianity evidentially and tackles some of the dilemmas of morality and some of the misconceptions about God. He includes in each chapter a witness list of credible people he would call to the stand were he to present the case for Christianity at a trial.

3. <u>Daniel: Prophet to the Nations</u>, Dr John M. Oakes, Illumination Publishers Intl.

    This is a well presented easy to understand book which was extremely helpful to me in gaining an understanding about the sheer weight of fulfilled biblical prophecy in the book of Daniel, especially so far as how much fulfilment came out of the influence of the Roman Empire

4. <u>Encountering the New Testament</u>, Walter A. Elwell & Robert W. Yarborough, Baker Books.

    Chapter 11 is a very good introduction to the modern study of the gospels.

5. The Reason for God, Timothy Keller, Hodder & Stoughton.

   Keller tackles some of the common objections from sceptics, such as how can a loving God send people to Hell? The church is responsible for so much injustice.

6. Evidence for the Historical Jesus, Josh McDowall & Bill Wilson, Harvest House Publishers.

   This is a must read for the subject of the historical Jesus. It is full of details and references to Jesus from ancient secular writers, a great deal of information about the early church leaders. Details on how we can be satisfied that the biblical records are reliable.

7. The New Testament Documents, 5th Ed, F.F.Bruce

   Short book which tackles the question, are the New Testament Documents reliable? Explains how the Bible canon was put together, when the Gospels first appeared, the importance of Paul's evidence are three key areas covered.

8. Compelling Evidence for God and the Bible, Douglas A Jacoby, 2010, Harvest House Publishers

   Tackles the main issues that build confidence in why we can trust the Bible. The reality of God, The Bible: the Word of God or the word of man? A very useful chapter on why we can be confident about the biblical manuscripts, even displays a location chart for the key manuscripts. From what I can see, this book is an expansion on a much earlier book by the same author, True and Reasonable, the very first apologetics book I read back in the 1990s and is very easy to follow.

9. Evidence that demands a Verdict, revised edition, Josh McDowall, Here's Life Publishers.

   A very detailed and in-depth analysis of historical evidence for Christianity. This book is a Christian apologetics classic. If you are only going to read one book on apologetics in your lifetime, read this one.

10. How to Read the Bible for All its Worth, by Gordon D. Fee & Douglas Stuart.

    A valuable aid to understanding the Bible and contextualising the narrative.

11. The Message of Daniel, Dale Ralph Davis, Inter Varsity Press.

    Ralph Davis explores the significant interpretative issues. The book is detailed and not as easy to digest as the book by Dr John Oakes, book number three on my bibliography. However, it is well worth reading.

12. The Mystery and Meaning of The Dead Sea Scrolls, Hershel Shanks, Random House

    Will greatly assist anyone wanting to gain knowledge of the most important archaeological find of the 20th Century. Not really relevant to the New Testament so not included in my narrative but invaluable when constructing an argument for the reliability of the Old Testament. Some relevance though as parts of the book of Daniel are amongst the Scrolls.

13. The History of Christianity, David Bentley Hart, Quercus Books.

    Provides an illustrated history of the Christian faith covering 2000 years.

14. The Historical Atlas of the Bible, Dr Ian Barnes

    Contains a helpful section on Alexander the Great that provides valuable background classic history to help the reader grasp the significance and accuracy of the Daniel prophecies.

15. Answers to Tough Questions, Josh McDowell & Don Stewart Here's Life Publishers inc, 1983.

    Tackles many of the tough questions sceptics ask about the Christian faith. Each chapter is short and concise. Health warning though, doctrine on how a person becomes a Christian appears to skip the important biblical instruction to be baptised.

16. Seeking Allah, Finding Jesus, Nabeel Qureshi, Zondervan, 2014.

A devout Muslim encounters Christianity. Chapter 34 is especially relevant to my own prologue. This is an excellent book and the reader gains helpful insights into the Islamic religion as they journey with Nabeel who converts to Christianity through the help of David Wood, a best friend at university. David Wood himself is now a well-known Christian apologist who devotes a lot of work into studying Islam and exploring where Islamic fundamentalist, obtain their beliefs. The book also provides a role model for how the Christian apologist can reach out to Muslim friends.

I recommend this book as an essential read. The read is especially poignant as Nabeel recently died at a young age due to stomach cancer so from the Christian believer's perceptive, David Wood (prominent in the book as they constantly spa together over their conflicting beliefs), through his persuasive outreach exposes him to the erroneous teachings of Islamic clerics concerning Christian doctrines, and leads him into the truth of salvation through Jesus Christ.

17. Intelligent Design, H Wayne House, Olive Tree Bible Software.

This was the key resource for my information in chapter 6 and formed the basis of how I presented Intelligent Design theory in Evidence For Conviction. The paper is a quick and easy read laying out the theory of I.D. very clearly making the narrative easy to follow.

Unused Material

This item did not make its way into the narrative of the book as it was a bit at odds with the flow of the chapters but I have retained it as unused material and include it here amongst my notes.

Beware of False Truths

One of the big problems in our society is just how swiftly fake news can circulate as accepted facts. This is especially the case with the rise of social media. I recall that very early into my conversion, I spent a bit of time with a friend of my brother, a Jamaican named Clifford. He was a very interesting character to speak to. He had dreadlocks but was not a Rastafarian. He spoke with a strong Jamaican accent and was very articulate

One of the things that impressed me about Clifford was how much he treasured the Bible. His own one was breaking at the seams and pages were falling out. We were engaged in a Bible study one day and he noticed that the book of Philemon was missing from his Bible. Philemon is the shortest book in the Bible, a letter by the Apostle Paul and only one page in length. Clifford was somewhat disconsolate about this loss and it distracted him from our study.

The next time we got together he triumphantly declared to me in his strong Jamaican accent and beaming smile, "I have found my piece of Philemon."

Something else he said to me rocked my boat a little bit. I was trying to reveal to him from scripture that he was not living the life of a disciple. At the end of the Bible study Clifford declared, "Anyway, the King James Bible is not the *real* Bible, the real Bible is the black man Bible, the Maccabean Bible. The white man banned it; you can't get it it's illegal in this country!"

I must say I was somewhat stumped by this and at that early stage with my knowledge of church history somewhat limited, I was a bit worried that I, along with the masses, had been hoodwinked into the mother of all religious conspiracies. I investigated the *black man's Bible* idea. What I discovered was that there simply was no evidence of a black man's Bible on the internet. However, I did find out that there were two ancient books, First Maccabees and second Maccabees.

These were two ancient texts that had been in existence from the inter-testament periods. That is the time between the Old and New Testaments. They were books of historical interest but did not add to or detract from the message of the gospels, or the Old Testament.

Those who have knowledge of church history will know that we have not always had the complete Bible as one combined book. From the 3rd century onwards the church strove to clarify what books were inspired of God, and to separate them from the other manuscripts in circulation. 1st and 2nd Maccabees were excluded from what eventually became accepted as the Bible Canon. The Maccabean texts did not make the cut and were left out.

It is my understanding however, that the Catholic Bible still includes the Maccabean texts. I satisfied myself that the Maccabean texts were not illegal. I have read them for myself. I managed to procure a copy of the Apocrypha from a charity shop and the books are contained inside. Had I not checked for myself and simply taken at face value what my articulate Jamaican friend had said, I would possibly have lost faith and worse still perpetuated this fake news. Do you see how facts can be twisted, misrepresented and even distorted? Yes, the Maccabean texts were excluded when the Bible was canonised, but these are by no means illegal and are readily available.

Sadly, there are far too many people today who hear things and embrace them as truth without testing the information. For example, have you heard it said, "Eye for an eye, tooth for a tooth." Was it suggested to you that this is demonstrative of

God's vengeful malevolent nature? However, if you read this text in its entirety and understand of the fact that the audience and culture at the time was big on dishing out justice and punishment, you soon understand that, what God was actually promoting, was nothing more than punishment to fit the crime. No more excessive retribution. Malevolent God or fair God? What do you think?

Recently I was speaking to Larry Samuels. He is a faithful brother in the Basildon Church of Christ, at the heart of everything we do even though he has some serious health concerns. I spoke to him about this *Black man's Bible* conspiracy theory. Larry was born and raised in Jamaica and he confirmed to me that the black man's Bible idea was something that was often spoken about in Jamaica when he was growing up.

Beware of miss-information.

www.ingramcontent.com/pod-product-compliance
Lightning Source LLC
Chambersburg PA
CBHW071623080526
44588CB00010B/1249